SAMURAI
WARRIOR

First published in June 2019

A catalogue record for this book is available from the
British Library.

ISBN 978 1 78521 562 9

Library of Congress control no. 2018953080

Published by Haynes Publishing,
Sparkford, Yeovil, Somerset
BA22 7JJ, UK.
Tel: 01963 440635
Int. tel: +44 1963 440635
Website: www.haynes.com

Haynes North America Inc.,
859 Lawrence Drive, Newbury Park,
California 91320, USA.

Printed in Malaysia.

All images are credited within the captions.

SAMURAI WARRIOR

OPERATIONS MANUAL

DAILY LIFE • FIGHTING TACTICS • RELIGION • ART • WEAPONS

CHRIS McNAB

CONTENTS

INTRODUCTION 6

CHAPTER 1 – HISTORY OF THE SAMURAI
THE RISE OF THE SHOGUNATE 12
EMPEROR VS SHOGUN 16
THE PERIOD OF WARRING STATES 20
THE EDO PERIOD 22
THE MEIJI RESTORATION 24

CHAPTER 2 – DWELLINGS AND DAILY LIFE
DWELLINGS 28
EVERYDAY DRESS 34
GROOMING 36
FOOD 38
DRINK 40
SAMURAI PASTIMES 43

CHAPTER 3 – SAMURAI SPIRITUALITY
THE RELIGIONS OF JAPAN 52
DEATH AND LOYALTY 60

CHAPTER 4 – SAMURAI ARMOUR AND EQUIPMENT
CLASSICAL-ERA ARMOUR 70
ARMOUR EVOLUTION, 15TH–17TH CENTURIES 78

CHAPTER 5 – WEAPONS AND FIGHTING SKILLS
THE SAMURAI ARSENAL 86
BOWS AND ARCHERY 88
NAGINATA 91
YARI 94
SAMURAI SWORDS 95
SWORD TRAINING AND FIGHTING TECHNIQUES 99
FIREARMS 102

CHAPTER 6 – SAMURAI ON CAMPAIGN
SOCIAL RANKS AND MOBILISATION 108
AN ARMY READY 110
THE MARCHING ARMY 114
LOGISTICS 120
FOOD AND RATIONS 124

CHAPTER 7 – THE SAMURAI IN BATTLE
STRUCTURE AND FORMATIONS 128
BATTLEFIELD COMMAND AND CONTROL 138
EXPERIENCE OF BATTLE 140

SELECT BIBLIOGRAPHY 152

ENDNOTES 153

INDEX 154

INTRODUCTION

Any analysis of a specific historical and cultural group needs to clarify its terms early on. Boiling the samurai down to its most essential property, we can classify this group as a military class or caste in the service of a specific lord and clan, each samurai giving his arms, organisation and wealth to the *daimyō* (lord of a ruling family) or the governing shogun (essentially a military dictator), although there was a special group of masterless samurai called *ronin* – we shall hear more from them later. The word samurai itself appears around the 10th century AD, in an anthology of poems called the *Kokin Wakashū* (905–14), but the term *bushi* – which is actually used synonymously with samurai – dates back to the previous century, and would be an interchangeable term throughout subsequent history. In translation, both terms roughly mean 'those who serve', as in serving a public cause, institution, leader or clan.

▼ *This photograph of a samurai, taken in the late 19th century, shows the warrior performing a downward strike with his* katana *sword. (Felice Beato/PD)*

HISTORICAL PRESENCE

During the period of their existence (c. 10th–19th century), the samurai were a central military, governmental and cultural force in Japan's history, although their status and relevance would undergo fluctuations and eventual decline. Indeed, as a social and military entity, the samurai have long disappeared from relevance. Although dark threads of samurai militarism were laced into Japanese nationalism during the 1920s, 30s and the apocalyptic years of World War II, albeit in a very historically contorted form, the decline of the samurai as a warrior class actually began back in the first decades of the 17th century, with the rise of the Tokugawa shogunate (see Chapter 1). From 1868, with the restoration of imperial rule and disappearance of the shogunate (under whose structures the samurai had largely been defined), Japan began its journey into modernity after two centuries of international

▼ *The great instructor of samurai sword fighting, Miyamoto Musashi, is featured here wielding two wooden* bokken *simultaneously. (Alkivar/CC-PD-Mark)*

isolationism, and the last samurai effectively disappeared from all but memory.

Yet the memory of the samurai, and what they are perceived to represent culturally, has turned out to be surprisingly durable. The samurai *way* – what has often come to be labelled as *bushidō* ('way of the warrior') – has proved deeply compelling to modern audiences on spiritual, aesthetic, martial and artistic levels. Updated or historically disinterred samurai warriors feature in hundreds of Hollywood epics, countless comic books, novels, business guides and self-help works, TV series and other forms of cultural expression. Why modern audiences are so attracted to such a culturally different and temporally deceased culture is a study rather beyond the remit of this book, though it is possible to say that the root cause is surely the manner in which the samurai represent, via the modern looking glass, a 'way' to transcend the anxiety and minutiae of modern daily life, through a unified philosophy of spirituality and discipline alongside a fearless martial spirit in the face of our own mortality.

CULTURAL UNDERSTANDING

Yet herein lies the problem. The successive cultural accretions that have been laid on top of actual samurai culture over the last century have made it hard to separate myth from reality when it comes to how the samurai lived and fought across eight centuries of Japanese history. If we look at the samurai during their periods of greatest influence (10th–17th centuries), the picture we draw can be far more nuanced than that of the noble and loyal warrior in popular circulation today.

▲ *Modern-day samurai re-enactors at the Odawara Hojo Godai Festival demonstrate arquebus fire at Odawara Castle in Kanagawa, Japan, 2009. (Robert Harding/Alamy)*

The samurai could be both disloyal and opportunistic at times, shifting their affiliations according to the prevailing political winds (although there are plenty of contrasting examples of devotion unto death). Not all samurai were masters of the martial crafts; some would have been more valued for their skills in administration and diplomacy than their ability to wield sword or bow. Indeed, during the Tokugawa period, the samurai were basically no more than a political class, the top 5–10 per cent of society dominating the financial structure of the nation. On the battlefield, the samurai were certainly a potent, and decisive, force, yet it was often the mass of *ashigaru* (peasant foot soldiers under service to land-owning samurai) who would come to decide the battle, especially with the arrival of firearms in Japan in the 16th century. Nor were all the samurai men; *onna-bugeisha*, trained female warriors, also took their place on the battlefield or served as armed guards to samurai households. The famous samurai sword was but one tool of combat, and arguably not the most important compared to samurai skills with bow and arrow. Finally, we need to balance our perceptions of the samurai as wise and judicious with their occasionally enormous capacity for casual cruelty. It was not uncommon for samurai armies to put entire populations to the sword or the flame, right down to infants. Skills in wielding the sword might be honed through killing commoners who were

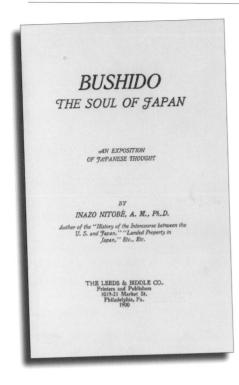

◄ Bushido, The Soul of Japan *(here seen in its first edition) did much to shape the idea of the samurai in the West, not always accurately.* (Houghton Library/ PD)

► *An image of samurai ferocity – Kojima Yatar, a warrior of the Sengoku period, carries a severed head in victory.* (Utagawa Kuniyoshi/ CC-PD-Mark)

perceived to have insulted the samurai, or executing criminals as an afternoon's diversion. Drawing on his memories of the 16th century, samurai clerk Yamamoto Tsunetomo stated: 'Last year I went to the Kase Execution Grounds to try my hand at beheading, and I found it to be an extremely good feeling.'

BUSHIDO

As we can see from the short list, the gulf between perception and reality when it comes to the samurai can be broad. Before we embark on a main analysis, furthermore, we must clarify our understanding of *bushidō*, as it is this concept that has underwritten much of our understanding about samurai.

Bushidō is actually a relatively modern term, its wellspring largely in the writings of Nitobe Inazō (1862–1933), produced in the late 1800s and early 1900s. Inazō very much represented new Japan, as a Christian educator, diplomat, politician, economist and writer, as well as being a senior figure in the emerging League of Nations. In 1900, Inazō published his most culturally influential work: *Bushido, The Soul of Japan: An Exposition of Japanese Thought*. Running to multiple editions, and published widely in English (in which language it arguably had more impact), the book was an effort to collect and identify the samurai's warrior code, and present it for the modern world. The writing is heavily Westernised in its style and range of literary references (Inazō studied, lived and worked for periods in the USA), and the following passage, taken from the early paragraphs of the book (13th edition), establishes his basic reasoning behind *bushidō*:

The Japanese word which I have roughly rendered Chivalry, is, in the original, more expressive than Horsemanship. *Bu-shi-do* means literally Military-Knight-Ways—the ways which fighting nobles should observe in their daily life as well as in their vocation; in a word, the 'Precepts of Knighthood,' the *noblesse oblige* of the warrior class. . . Bushido, then, is the code of moral principles which the knights were required or instructed to observe. It is not a written code; at best it consists of a few maxims handed down from mouth to mouth or coming from the pen of some well-known warrior or savant. More frequently it is a code unuttered and unwritten, possessing all the more the powerful sanction of veritable deed, and of a law written on the fleshly tablets of the heart. It was founded not on the creation of one brain, however able, or on the life of a single personage, however renowned. It was an organic growth of decades and centuries of military career.[1]

Inazō is right to say that there is no definitive samurai code in written form. There are some texts that have become landmarks of samurai thinking and tactics, certainly. The *Hagakure* is one, as is Miyamoto Musashi's *The Book of Five Rings* (c. 1645) and Yagyū Munemori's *Family Traditions on the Art of War* (1632), alongside major collections of texts and sayings from great samurai warriors, particularly the codifications that took place under the Tokugawa shogunate, including the *Zōhyō Monogatari* (Tales of the Foot Soldiers) and the scrolls of Natori Masazumi for the Natori-ryu school of warfare. These documents do give us an insight into the principles under which the samurai lived and fought, which indeed had a high degree of commonality. Yet Inazō's concept of *bushidō* took on something of a life of its own, giving the impression that it was a single set of rules for life that governed all samurai behaviour. In the work, he identified seven key virtues practised by the samurai:

- Rectitude or Justice
- Courage, the Spirit of Daring or Bearing
- Benevolence, the Feeling of Distress
- Politeness
- Veracity or Truthfulness
- Honour
- The Duty of Loyalty

All of these qualities were bound together in 'that discipline of disciplines, Self-Control', in which 'Calmness of behavior, composure of mind, should not be disturbed by passion of any kind.' He also placed the sword as the physical embodiment of the samurai's spirituality – 'the Soul of the Samurai' – although its use was to be guided by all the virtues and self-discipline above.

Inazō's study is full of grandeur and passion, an attempt both to define the samurai's moral compass and make this compass relevant to the modern age. He finishes the work by stating that: 'Bushido as an independent code of ethics may vanish, but its power will not perish from the earth; its schools of martial prowess or civic honor may be demolished, but its light and its glory will long survive their ruins.'

Ironically, it is his codification of *bushidō* that to a large extent preserved samurai culture in popular thought. Other subsequent movements did more work in this regard, such as the resurgence of interest in martial arts in the West during the 1970s. Yet it is not entirely accurate, being a heavily romanticised picture of what Inazō *wanted* the samurai to be, rather than what they were. To understand samurai culture properly, we cannot extract it from the time and locale in which it was enacted. Being a samurai was not a transcendent faith, crossing time immutably. As this book will show, the samurai were a diverse and evolving warrior class united, if we focus with a wide field of view, by certain traditions, tactics, weapons, governance and ways of living. In the following pages, we will both try to do justice to what united the samurai and to what made them different over time and space.

▼ *In this colourised photograph, taken in 1892, we see a variety of samurai weaponry and paraphernalia. Note the contrasting armour styles. (T. Enami/PD)*

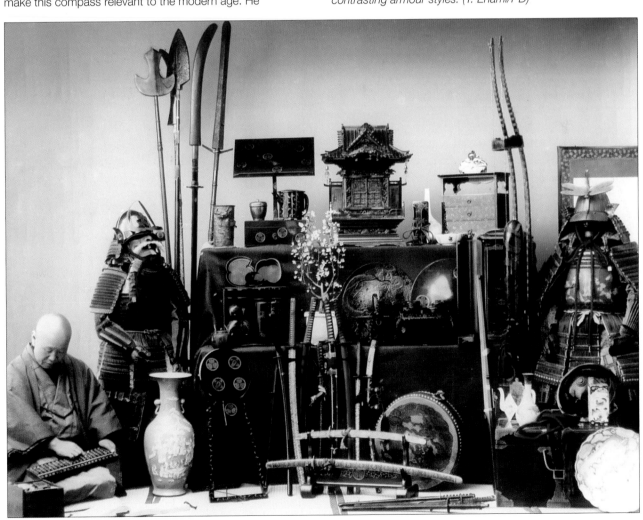

CHAPTER ONE

HISTORY OF THE SAMURAI

The samurai emerge into history, at least in terms of explicit references, in the 10th century AD. Japan was by this time a territory ruled over, albeit often precariously, by an imperial line that had established itself roughly by the 6th century. Japan was, and remained throughout our history, a nation of clans and regional families, with their own power bases, bureaucracies, wealth and armies, the latter warrior-like and belligerent. A central motif of samurai history was the struggle for clans to assert themselves in relation to those around them, expanding their power either through geographical conquest or through sage alliances. They also had to establish their relationship successfully, or otherwise, with those above them, from the *daimyō* lords up to the ruling shogun or emperor. It was a situation that was to give Japanese history a brutal fluidity, once that wasn't entirely controlled until the ascent of the Tokugawa shogunate in the 17th century.

◄ *An Edo period Japanese screen depicts the Battle of Sekigahara (21 October 1600), the clash that enabled the establishment of the Tokugawa shogunate. (Collection of The City of Gifu Museum of History/CC-PD)*

THE RISE OF THE SHOGUNATE

Much of Japanese history is dominated by rising warlords jostling against imperial power. From the late 12th century, the *shōgun* became the greatest of those warlords, exceeding even the Emperor in authority. The position of the shogunate, however, could be a precarious one in a time of intense political and military manoeuvring.

NARA AND HEIAN PERIODS (710–1192)

From the clan struggles of the early medieval period, a dominant imperial line was eventually established, known as the Yamato, and in 710 Yamato rulers established their capital city in Nara, although this was moved to Kyoto in 894. The shift to Kyoto ushered in what is called the Heian period – Kyoto was originally called Heian-kyō. The Yamato court was heavily Sino-centric in its customs and governmental models, Chinese culture and religion having flowed into Japan from the 6th century. As with all empires of this age, the Yamato court was also riddled with intrigue and scheming. Of all the powerful families in Japan at this time, the Fujiwara had the most muscle, its family members progressively taking over positions within the Yamato government, resulting in the rebellion of Taira no Masakado (d. 940) of the Kanmu Taira clan, who led a five-year revolt against the imperial court and even proclaimed himself a new emperor.

The 'Tenkei Rebellion' was eventually quashed with military force, but from this effort the samurai started to take their more central place in Japanese political machinations, as the warriors attached to the powerful families became instruments by which the emperor or regional lords could repress unruly subjects. Following the rebellion, two especially commanding families came to dominate much of Japanese politics and society: the Minamoto and the Taira. Through two localised wars – the Hōgen Insurrection of 1156 and the Heiji Insurrection of 1160 – the Taira took ascendancy, effectively removing the Fujiwara from imperial court influence, and replacing it with their own, and killing both Minamoto no Yoshitomo (an imperial provincial governor) and Fujiwara no Nobuyori, who had been in line to become regent to the emperor. (One factor that precipitated all manner of friction and conflict in Japanese politics was the regular appointment of regents to manage the affairs of junior emperors or, later, shoguns. Regents were capable of enormous misuse of power and privilege, effectively reducing the nominal ruler to a mere puppet.) In a humane decision that would reverberate throughout Japanese history, however, Taira no Kiyomori, the leader of the Taira, spared the lives of the young Minamoto boys, Yoshitsune and Yoritomo. The consequences of that action would lead future samurai commanders to be far less compassionate.

▼ *A group of bow-armed mounted Japanese samurai patrol the coastline during the Mongolian incursion of 1281. (Lebrecht Music & Arts/Alamy)*

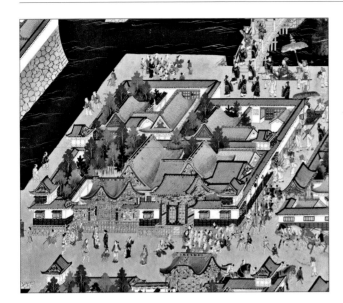

▲ *A scene of the city of Edo in the 17th century. From a small fishing village, it grew to be a city of more than one million people. (Marku1988/PD).*

THE GENPEI WAR (1180–85)

The fault lines that ran between the Taira and the Minamoto only widened with time. In 1180, Japan's Prince Mochihito, angered by Kiyomori's manipulation of succession to the imperial throne, secretly worked with the now-adult Minamoto no Yoritomo, agreeing that if the Minamoto could defeat and overthrow the Taira, Mochihito would become emperor. (The emperor at this time, following the abdication of Emperor Takakura, was Antoku, Kiyomori's two-year-old grandson.) Yoritomo, looking to avenge the past, rallied an army of followers, and went to war. This five-year conflict would be known as the Genpei War, derived from the Chinese reading of the names Minamoto (*gen*) and Taira (*hei*); the Taira were also referred to as the Heike, and the Minamoto as the Genji.

The Genpei War had a fundamental shaping effect upon subsequent Japanese history, and upon that of the samurai. The war demonstrated that it was military power that would define the future of imperial and clan relations, and the samurai were at the vanguard, supported on occasions by the muscle of the *sohei*, religious warrior armies (see feature box).

The first action of the Genpei War was fought at Uji, just outside Kyoto, on 20 June 1180, with Minamoto no Yorimasa and Prince Mochihito at the head of a small force that largely consisted of a few hundred *sohei* from the temple of Todai-ji. The Minamoto, fleeing from a larger Taira army, crossed a bridge over the Uji River, ripping up the planks after them to prevent the Taira crossing, or at least crossing easily. That action, plus the bravura fighting spirit of certain *sohei*, such as the grandly named 'Tajima the Arrow Cutter', became the stuff of legend, but it could not prevent the Minamoto's first decisive defeat. Even as his sons Nakatsuna and Kanetsuna were fighting to the death, Yorimasa committed *seppuku* (suicide by disembowelment) and Mochihito was captured

THE *SOHEI*

From the 10th century, Japan had seen the growth of what were in effect private religious armies. Alongside the growth of Buddhism, and its division into rival sects, many monasteries felt the need to develop their own guard units, to protect the order from criminal raiding parties and to enforce their way during battles with opposing monasteries; religion was both militant and militarised during this period of Japan's history. The first such force was created in 970 at the temple of Enryaku-ji, a Tendai monastery located on Mount Hiei, near Kyoto, but others soon followed. Guard units grew into forces of army size and status – the Mount Hiei army soon numbered several thousand – and were known as *sohei*, or 'warrior monks', although a significant percentage of the forces would likely be composed of mercenaries. During the Genpei War, the *sohei* became important tools in the struggle between the Taira and Minamoto, the temples allying themselves to one side or the other, and occasionally switching their allegiances, although at the beginning of the war the *sohei* were primarily faithful to the Minamoto. There was a cost to this eschewing transcendence in favour of militarism: many of the temples, including that on Mount Hiei in 1180, were destroyed in the subsequent fighting.

▼ *A 19th-century print depicts two samurai fighting on the roof of a tower. The warrior on the left appears to be wielding a closed war fan or dagger. (Science History Images/Alamy)*

and killed. Todai-ji was put to the torch. It was clear that the Genpei War was going to be fought without mercy. To give the Minamoto some succour, Kiyomori died of illness shortly afterwards. Minamoto no Yoritomo took over at the head of the Minamoto campaign, supported by his brother Yoshitsune and his cousin Minamoto Kiso no Yoshinaka.

During the first months of the Genpei War, the Taira were in the ascendant. Yoritomo suffered a major defeat at the Battle of Ishibashiyama in September 1180, the Minamoto army thrown off balance and routed by a night attack from 3,000 Taira troops, led by Ōba Kagechika. Yoritomo escaped, but further Minamoto defeats followed, at Sunomata and Yahagigawa in 1181 and Hiuchi in 1183. But then, in June 1183, came the turning point in the war, the Battle of Kurikara. Yoshinaka was in charge of a numerically inferior Minamoto army; the Taira forces were up to eight times greater in size. Yet through several brilliant acts of deception, in which Yoshinaka convinced the Taira commanders that the Minamoto forces were far larger than they actually were, plus some intelligent manoeuvring, Yoshinaka ambushed the Taira in the Kurikara Pass, routing the enemy and achieving a brilliant victory.

Kurikara set the Taira on a path from which they did not recover. Several further critical defeats followed, including more in which Yoshinaka commanded the Minamoto army (the battles of Shinowara, Mizushima and Fukuryūji). Yoshinaka's reputation and self-confidence were growing, which in the age of the samurai often meant a hubris ripe for subsequent downfall. For the Minamoto, the battle produced some unforeseen internal problems. Yoshinaka, flushed with his victories, saw fit to name himself *sei-i taishōgun* (the origin of the shortened shogun title), which implied he was now commander-in-chief of the Minamoto, and set himself up as ruler in Kyoto (the Taira and the infant emperor had fled by this time). Yoritomo, meanwhile, had established his own base of authority in Kamakura; it was clear that the two men were in essence developing rival courts. The tension eventually spilled over into outright hostility, and eventually

▲ *Samurai Saigo Takamori (1827–77) commits* seppuku, *or ritual suicide, during the Satsuma Rebellion. (Granger Historical Picture Archive/Alamy)*

Yoshinaka was driven from Kyoto and was killed at the Battle of Awazu in February 1184.

The internecine struggles between Yoritomo and Yoshinaka by no means reprieved the Taira from their escalating collapse. Following Awazu, there were several further battles that sealed the Taira's fate, culminating in the great sea engagement at Dan-no-Ura in 1185, in which the last-stand Taira army was defeated so decisively that many of the Taira samurai simply threw themselves off the ships, preferring suicide by drowning to the ignominy of ultimate defeat.

The Minamoto emerged as the ultimate victors of the Genpei War, and Yoritomo immediately set out to consolidate his power. With ruthless intent, he first turned upon his younger brother Yoshitsune, who had largely been responsible for many of the Minamoto victories once Yoshinaka had been removed from the scene. Powered by jealousy (Yoshitsune had been awarded several titles by Emperor Go-Shirakawa) and family squabbles, Yoritomo's army hunted down Yoshitsune, and at the Battle of Koromogawa he was killed, along with his ever-faithful *sohei* companion, Benkei.

THE SHOGUNATE

In the aftermath of the Genpei War, we perhaps enter the true age of the samurai; for a profound political change now occurred in Japan, one that would shape its history until the 19th century. In 1192, Minamoto Yoritomo took the title of shogun, as head of a state military government known as a *bakufu* (lit. 'tent government'). The new government was based at Kamakura in what is today Kanagawa Prefecture, and it ushered in what has been called the Kamakura period, which ran from 1185 to 1333.

The rise of the Kamakura *bakufu* reshaped the established order of Japan. The emperor was still on the throne, but his

▲ *A detail from the 'Heiji scroll' depicts the Heiji Insurrection of 1160, the first major clash between the Minamoto and Taira clans. (Heritage Image Partnership Ltd/Alamy)*

position was now toothless and largely ceremonial – it was Yoritomo who held actual power. Furthermore, the shogunate was given a hereditary succession within the Minamoto family, making the position a dynastic one. To rule over his disputatious and scattered territories, Yoritomo gave his lords across Japan a high degree of autonomy to rule as they saw fit, their authority heavily derived from the army of samurai and peasant foot soldiers they had at their command. The combination of a militaristic shogunate, a feudal and clan-based social structure, and the presence of regional armies

tied in service to their lords cemented the samurai as an elite class within Japanese society at large.

Power did not, however, bring peace. Yoritomo died from a riding accident in 1199, and there followed a sequence of regencies within the shogunate, mirroring the imperial way of getting around inconveniently young monarchs. These were less than successful. The next emperor, Yoritomo's young son Yoriie was basically imprisoned and eventually assassinated by his fiercely ambitious mother Masako and grandfather Hōjō Tokimasa. His successor, Yoriie's 12-year-old brother Sanetomo, also came under the cruel wing of Tokimasa (it was now that Tokimasa officially established the role of *shikken*, or regent), and although he reached adulthood, he too was assassinated, in his mid-20s. The issue of succession, as Minamoto candidates ran out, eventually flared up into conflict between Tokimasa and Emperor Go-Toba, which only served to reinforce the shogunate after Go-Toba was defeated in 1221 and Kyoto was occupied by the forces of the *bakufu*.

◄ *A line artwork of a samurai in full battle uniform, including the sashimono identifier on his back. (Granger Historical Picture Archive/Alamy)*

► *A depiction of Watanabe no Tsuna (953–1025), a samurai, a retainer of Minamoto no Yorimitsu, battling Ibaraki-doji, a notorious Oni. (Science History Images/Alamy)*

EMPEROR VS SHOGUN

During the remainder of the 13th century, Japan experienced a measure of internal peace, the greatest threats coming from without, in the form of the Mongol invasions (see feature box). The shogunate went through a succession of regencies, now with the Hōjō rather than the Minamoto being the dominant family line.

The war against the Mongols resulted, on both occasions, in Japanese victories (assisted tremendously by fortuitous weather conditions), but the conflict actually weakened the *bakufu* economically, not least through the need to pay so many samurai for their service.

At this moment, a new emperor – Go-Daigo, crowned in 1318 – sensed an opportunity for imperial power to reassert itself over the *bakufu*, and thus began the Nanbokuchō Wars, or 'Wars between the Courts'. Go-Daigo was supported in his ambitions by the talented commander Kusunoki Masashige.

THE MONGOL INVASIONS

In 1274, the warrior leader of the Mongols, the infamous Kublai Khan, looked to expand his already massive empire beyond the Eurasian mainland, specifically eastwards across to Japan. As was the Mongol custom, threatening diplomacy was tried first; he wrote to the *bakufu* regent Hōjō Tokimune demanding that the Japanese pay his tribute. Samurai defiance returned a negative response, so in 1274 the Mongols (with additional Chinese and Korean troops) sent an invasion fleet of c. 20,000 men in 800 ships, landing them on Kyushu in the south of the Japanese island chain.

The Mongol invasion introduced the samurai to a very different style of warfare. The Mongols used crude and brutal mass-infantry tactics, the shock of scale clashing with the samurai's focus on more formal and elite combat. There were some initial significant defeats for the Japanese – at Tsushima Island, Iki Island, Hirado Island and others – but the Mongols nonetheless were surprised by the sheer tenacity of the samurai resistance. Just as the Mongol casualties and thinning logistics were beginning to bite, the Japanese took two victories at Akasaka and Torikei-Gate. The beleaguered Mongols eventually retreated to their ships at Hakata harbour, looking to relocate their troops, when they were hit by a massive typhoon that wiped out dozens

of ships and thousands of men. The invasion therefore failed, with the loss of some 13,000 Mongol troops.

After six years of recovery, the Mongols decided to have another go at Japan, in 1281. Now understanding the level of Japanese resistance, the Mongols put together an even greater army – more than 140,000 men in 4,000 ships. It sailed for Hakata Bay, scene of their earlier destruction by maelstrom, but the Japanese had predicted this move, and in the intervening years had constructed large defensive walls and works around the coastline.

The khan's fleet did not arrive around Kyushu as one mass entity, but rather in staggered waves. The first Chinese fleet, about 40,000 troops in 900 ships, sailed from Masan, Korea, and landed at Tsushima Island on 21 May. The battlegrounds for the invasion were largely the same as before, but this time the Mongols suffered a succession of defeats from the outset in May–July, inflicted by the well-prepared Japanese and assisted by the spread of disease through the Mongol soldiers and ships' crews. The larger Mongol fleet, 100,000 men strong, then arrived to face Japanese defenders already weakened by the combat of previous days. However, on 15 August, nature intervened again on Japan's behalf. A monstrous storm, later called *kamikaze* (divine wind), virtually wiped out the Mongol fleet while it sat at anchor. Only about one-third of the invasion force survived, and limped home. Although a third invasion was argued for by Kublai Khan, this was never implemented, and Japan remained free of foreign invaders.

▼ *Scenes of naval combat during the Mongolian invasion of 1281, with samurai boarding Chinese ships plus utilising their long-range archery skills. (CC-PD-Mark)*

▶ *Emperor Go-Daigo took the imperial throne between 1318 and 1339. His reign was notable for pushing back against the power of the shogun, overthrowing the Kamakura shogunate in 1333. (CC-PD-Mark)*

It was a complicated conflict, as were many Japanese wars of our study. At first, Go-Daigo was on the back foot, being compelled to flee Kyoto in 1331, although Masashige's skills in a form of guerrilla warfare managed to keep the shogun's armies from decisive victory. Then, in a major blow for the Hōjō, two of their commanders, Ashikaga Takauji and Nitta Yoshisada, effectively swapped sides. Takauji occupied Kyoto while Yoshisada attacked and took Kamakura itself in July 1333, overthrowing the *bakufu*. Yet Takauji, dissatisfied with what he saw as meagre rewards for his loyalty, then himself marched on Kamakura, and proceeded in an attempt to set up his own *bakufu* government.

The result was another spate of combat, with Nitta Yoshisada and Kusunoki Masashige on one side, representing Go-Daigo, and the Ashikaga on the other. At Minatogawa on 4 July 1336, the Ashikaga secured a resounding victory, both Yoshisada and Masashige being killed. In triumph,

▼ *The siege of Akasaka Castle in 1331 was an early battle in the Genkō War. The castle was held by Kusunoki Masashige, for Emperor Go-Daigo. (World History Archive/Alamy)*

▲ *A statue of Kusunoki Masashige (1294–1336), whose loyalty to the emperor eventually led to his defeat at Minatogawa in 1336. (David Moore/CC-BY-SA-2.5)*

▲ *Ashikaga Takauji (1305–58) was the first of the Ashikaga shoguns, and both a warrior and a diplomat in equal measures. (Urashimataro/PD-Art).*

Takauji went to Kyoto and established what he saw as a new imperial line. For half a century, Japan had two rival imperial courts: the northern court at Kyoto (the Ashikaga *bakufu*) and the southern court under Go-Daigo, now at Yoshino near Nara. In the early 1390s, however, the southern court folded and the Ashikaga would thereafter rule the country.

THE ASHIKAGA SHOGUNATE

While the Ashikaga's nominee for emperor became the established imperial line, the *bakufu* was consolidated. The seat of the shogunate was in the Muromachi district of Tokyo, and thus the period from 1336 to 1573, the final year being that in which the last Ashikaga shogun of the line was expelled from Kyoto, is now referred to as the Muromachi period. This era was significant for the further social ascent of the samurai. The turbulence of the Nanbokuchō period had deepened the need for lords to cement the loyalty of their samurai. Only with a samurai who was deeply committed to the well-being of the clan could a lord preserve his future power, and thus the relationship between commander and

◀ *The Battle of Mikata ga Hara in 1573 saw the forces of Takeda Shingen inflict a rare defeat on those of Tokugawa Ieyasu and Oda Nobunaga. (Utagawa Yoshitora/ CC-PD-Mark)*

samurai became a very definite two-way street. The lords of the Muromachi period were given the title *shugo*, effectively military governors. They wielded considerable power within their own domains, and the shogunate would always have an eye over one shoulder to see how the *shugo* aligned their loyalties, and therefore their armies.

Although the rise of the Ashikaga *bakufu* largely settled the imperial frictions of the past, there were always other wars to be fought. During the 15th century, for example, the *shugo* faced a series of rebellions from the Ikko-ikki ('single-minded ones'), militant Buddhist groups allied to the Jōdo Shinshū sect, formed from disaffected and leaderless samurai, peasant warriors, farmers and townspeople. These ad hoc armies collected together to resist what they saw as the excesses of feudal rule, and it would take until the late 16th century for their power and spirit to be finally crushed.

Importantly, however, the demonstration of the power of low-ranking foot soldiers was instructive to the *shugo*, who now began to recruit their own non-samurai armies, called *ashigaru*. The *ashigaru*, combined with the introduction of matchlock firearms into Japan in the 16th century, ultimately supplanted the samurai as the leading tactical force, steadily replacing the samurai at the vanguard on the battlefield. Indeed, such became their status and influence that many *ashigaru*, by the 17th century, had elided into the samurai class themselves, a minor social revolution in feudal Japan. Samurai historian Anthony Bryant perfectly captures the implications: 'The increasing size of an armed and militarily trained lower class was setting the stage for what came to be called *gokokujo*: the low overcoming the high. It was a dangerous time to be weak.'[2]

In 1467, Japan saw the outbreak of what is known as the Ōnin War, a clash of ultimately devastating consequences. A dispute over succession to the shogunate of Ashikaga

▲ *Rōnin warriors, the legendary '47 Rōnin', storm the house of court official Kira Yoshinaka. Rōnin became more numerous during the Edo period. (Katsushika Hokusai/CC-PD-Mark)*

Yoshimasa (the eighth Ashikaga shogun) brought out rivalries between two clans, the Yamana and the Hosokawa. With the terrible logic of martial escalation, the conflict grew and spread. It lasted for ten years, and resulted in the near destruction of Kyoto and, crucially, the critical weakening of the Ashikaga *bakufu*.

▼ *Katō Kiyomasa (1562–1611), a samurai warrior of great renown, hunting tigers in Korea during the Imjim War. (Tsukioka Yoshitoshi/CC-PD-Mark)*

THE PERIOD OF WARRING STATES

The Sengoku *jidai* – the Period of the Warring States – is in many ways the core of samurai history. In terms of periodisation, the era lasted well over a century, from c. 1467 to c. 1600. With the authority of the shogun fatally undermined, the centre could not hold, and Japan's internal relations descended into a contest of military supremacy.

The *shugō* now became the *daimyō* – regional feudal lords with their own armies, loyalties and agendas – and in the absence of a shogun – they now fought for their own interests and power. Thus, for some 130 years, Japan descended into an interminable string of ghastly wars, the shifting sands of victories, defeats and loyalties meaning that one war quickly laid the ground for the next. The samurai and the emergent *ashigaru* were in constant violent employment; this period alone helps us to understand the samurai spiritual preoccupation with matters of death and dying. It was a true dark ages, with no certainty, and rule through the sword.

Tracing the detailed history of the Sengoku *jidai* is impossible here, such was its complexity. We should, however, acknowledge some of the great *daimyō* and clans who emerged during this time, a handful of whom came to be the embodiment of samurai virtues, command skills and military ruthlessness. Luminaries include the *daimyō* Takeda Shingen (1521–73), Hōjō Uijyasu (1515–70) and Uesugi Kenshin (1530–78). But two men above all others served to lead Japan out of its interminable internecine warfare and bring about the reunification of the state: Oda Nobunaga and Tokugawa Ieyasu.

The son of Oda Nobuhide, a minor *daimyō* in Owari Province, Oda Nobunaga was talented in all the key samurai skills – politics, diplomacy and war fighting. His focus was on bringing Japan's scattered conflicts under his unification. Militarily, Nobunaga was the man to do this. An innovator, he was one of the first *daimyō* to create an army that fully integrated the musket-armed *ashigaru* into the forefront of

▼ *A ferocious close-up of the great Takeda Shingen (1521–73). Note the distinguishing horned* mae date *crest attached to the front of the helmet. (Utagawa Kuniyoshi/PD-Art)*

▼ *The* daimyō *Uesugi Kenshin (1530–78) was a dominant military and political figure during the Sengoku period. (Utagawa Kuniyoshi/PD-Art)*

PROMINENT *DAIMYŌ* OF THE SENGOKU *JIDAI*

▲ *The Battle of Kawanakajima in 1561. The samurai forces of Takeda Shingen are on the left and those of Uesugi Kenshin are on the right. (Hiroshige/CC-PD-Mark)*

Takeda Shingen (1521–73) – Born in Kai province, originally named Takeda Harunobu, Takeda Shingen forced his father to resign as the head of the clan in 1541, after which time he focused on aggressive military expansion out from the clan-controlled Kai Province into Shinano and then the Kanto. Thus, he came into conflict with both the Hōjō and Uesugi, fighting the latter (led by Uesugi Kenshin) no fewer than five times at Kawanakajima. Shingen rose to dominate east-central Japan, and even managed to defeat the army of Tokugawa Ieyasu in 1573 at Hamamatsu. Shingen died of natural causes that same year, and the combined armies of Nobunaga and Ieyasu crushed Takeda power when they defeated Shingen's son, Katsuyori, at Nagashino in 1575.

Hōjō Uijyasu (1515–70) – *Daimyō* of the Odawara Hōjō clan, Hōjō Uijyasu was the son of Hōjō Ujitsuna, who had already locked horns with the Uesugi in Kanto, major Hōjō victories including the battles of Edo Castle (1524) and Konōdai (1538). In the 1560s, Uijyasu led his armies against the threat from Takeda Shingen, one of the greatest engagements being that at Odawara Castle in 1569, which Shingen burned to the ground before withdrawing. Eventually, Ujiyasu made peace treaties with both Uesugi Kenshin and Takeda Shingen.

Uesugi Kenshin (1530–78) – Originally named Nagao Torachiyo, Uesugi Kenshin was born into a powerful family in Echigo Province, a family that in the 1540s fell on harder times with the death of the father. Kenshin changed his surname and allegiance to Uesugi in 1552, when sheltering Uesugi Norimasa following the Uesugi's defeat by the Hōjō. Kenshin had previously been Norimasa's vassal, but Norimasa now adopted him as a son, giving Kenshin great power that he wielded with expertise, although he was ultimately unable to achieve a decisive victory over Takeda Shingen. Kenshin died in 1578, even as he was planning a campaign against Oda Nobunaga.

battlefield tactics. Nobunaga was also capable of making excellent alliances, not least with Tokugawa Ieyasu, the *daimyō* from Mikawa Province and another commander of talent and vision.

Nobunaga was more than just a tactician: he had a sage understanding of the role of finance in warfare, abolishing road tolls and the fees collected from trade guilds, for example, thereby starving rival *daimyō* of some of their principal means of filling the war coffers. Whenever Nobunaga acquired a new territory, furthermore, he made judicious investments in the local samurai, rewarding them for their new allegiance and thus growing his power base.

Together, Nobunaga and Ieyasu were unstoppable. In the late 1560s, Nobunaga took over Kyoto and abolished the Ashikaga shogunate, and by the 1580s all of central Japan and much of western Japan was under his power. In 1582, however, Nobunaga felt compelled to commit *seppuku* after one of his retainers wounded him in an assassination attempt.

THE EDO PERIOD

Nobunaga's shoes were filled by one of his generals, Toyotomi Hideyoshi, who continued the military work of bringing Japan into line. Capitalising on the fact that Nobunaga had left him a massive military force and effective systems of political control, Hideyoshi achieved landmark victories at battles such as Yamazaki (1582) and Shizugatake (1583), and by 1591 he had brought all of Japan under his control.

Of note is that Hideyoshi was actually of *ashigaru* (foot soldier) rank – a prime example of *gokokujō* (overthrowing one's superiors). The Sengoku *jidai* was nearly, but not quite, over.

Tokugawa Ieyasu had served under Hideyoshi as under Nobunaga, but in 1584 the ambitious Ieyasu – always looking ahead to the top job – fought Hideyoshi's forces at Nagakute, although the two men subsequently negotiated in favour of Hideyoshi's continued rule, which included the title *kanpaku*, essentially the chief advisor to the emperor. Yet Ieyasu was a patient man. Hideyoshi died in 1598, his leadership significantly undermined by disastrous campaigning in Korea. His son Hideyori took the reins of power, but Japan was now dividing again between those allied to Ieyasu and those who stuck with Hideyori.

On 21 October 1600, Ieyasu fought Hideyori's army (commanded by Ishida Mitsunari) at Sekigahara. In a brilliant victory, Ieyasu took the field, and thus became the undisputed ruler of Japan, a fact cemented by his adoption of the title of shogun in 1603, centred on Edo.

Despite some military challenges to the Tokugawa shogunate in the first half of the 17th century, Japan was now entering a time of durable peace, which lasted from 1603 until 1868. The Tokugawa achieved their stability through a mix of carrot and stick. Loyalty from the *daimyō* to the shogun brought them wealth and social standing, but the Alternate

▲ *Toyotomi Hideyoshi, seen here in contemplative mood, is famed for having unified Japan, largely bringing it out of a long period of internecine warfare. (CC-PD-Mark)*

◄ *A statue of Oda Nobunaga in Kiyosu Park, Japan. Large sections of sode armour protect his upper arms and shoulders. (Bariston/ CC-BY-SA-4.0)*

▼ *A maki-e go game board at the Ryōgen, in the temple at Daitoku-ji, Kyoto, Japan; the board was used by Toyotomi Hideyoshi and Tokugawa Ieyasu. (Fg2/PD-Self)*

▶ *An impressive Japanese screen depicting the Battle of Sekigahara. Note how the standards and banners bring some measure of coherence to the battlefield. (CC-PD-Mark)*

Attendance System – in which the *daimyō* families were to all intents and purposes kept as polite hostages in Edo – hinted at the consequences of defiance. Other laws enforced strict controls over the actions of the local lords. In the Exclusion Edict of 1639, furthermore, Japan severed virtually all contact with the outside world, meaning that the codes, structures and tactics of old would remain under a historical glass bell jar, preserved from foreign influence.

The other consequence of the Tokugawa rule was actually the beginning of the end of the samurai. During the Sengoku *jidai*, fighting skills had been at a premium, and those skills through experience had been kept as sharp as the samurai swords. However, under a long period of peace, those skills began to wither. The samurai continued to practise and preach the warrior code – indeed, many of the key writings of samurai instruction come from the Edo period, and the great *daimyō* still exercised themselves with keeping and supporting huge armies, marching to Edo on an annual basis in lavish displays of armour, weaponry and manpower. Despite this, steadily, much of the samurai's life became focused on administration and governance, rather than severing enemy's heads in battle.

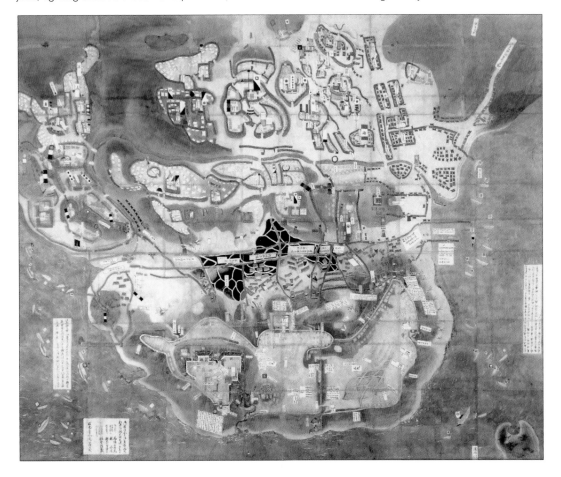

◀ *An anonymous 17th-century Japanese map depicting the Siege of Hara Castle, fought in 1637–38 during the Shimabara Rebellion. (CC-PD-Mark)*

THE MEIJI RESTORATION

The final curtain in the samurai drama essentially began to fall in 1852, when four US ships commanded by one Commodore Matthew Perry appeared off the coast of Japan, demanding that the country open itself up through a trade treaty.

By this time, the Tokugawa shogunate was already in decline, unsettled by economic problems, a rising entrepreneurial class, peasant unrest from crop failures, widespread poverty, natural disasters and probing intrusions from European and Russian traders. Japan, facing a modern armed force with only smouldering matchlocks and outdated blades, was compelled to open its doors. Turbulence followed in the country as the Tokugawa tried to reassert itself, but all in vain. The reformist Emperor Meiji took imperial rule in 1867 (it would last until 1912), and by 1870 the shogunate had been abolished, flickerings of Tokugawa resistance quashed at the Battle of Hakodate (1868–69).

The samurai were now a dying class. In 1871, the domains of the *daimyō* – the essence of the feudal system under which the samurai survived – were abolished, the *daimyō* and the samurai being effectively paid off. In 1873, military conscription was introduced, with a compulsory four years of in-uniform service and three years in the reserve for all young adult men. Given that previously the samurai had been the only class allowed to carry weapons, it was transparent that

▼ *Pictured during the Siege of Osaka in 1614–15, these mostly mounted samurai are principally armed with extremely long* yumi *(bows). (J Marshall, Tribaleye Images/Alamy)*

▲ Rebel samurai (right) engage government troops in 1877 at the Battle of Tabaruzaka. Although we see much gunfire, rain actually dampened the weapons. (Sensai Eitaku/CC-PD-Mark)

▼ Last acts of the samurai tradition. Japanese soldiers surrender their swords to Allied troops at the end of World War II. (Military Images/Alamy)

the samurai were now anachronistic in the age of mass armies recruited mainly from the ranks of the working and middle classes.

There was some pushback. In January 1877, the Satsuma Rebellion saw a large-scale revolt by samurai warriors, which lasted an impressive nine months. However, against an increasingly modern and swelling national army, the samurai cause was futile, and after some major battlefield defeats the rebellion petered out.

The age of the samurai was now emphatically over. Its spirit lingered on, however, in literature, myth and art. It also persisted, albeit in a warped form, in the militaristic nationalism of the 1920s–40s. In 1945, for example, bewildered US troops on battlegrounds such as Iwo Jima and Okinawa watched units of Japanese infantry make futile suicide charges, the officer at the front often clutching his samurai sword high above his head, screaming his fury before being cut down in hails of modern small-arms fire. In some minor way, the samurai spirit has also persisted in modern martial arts, which aspire (with many degrees of imperfection) to similar codes of discipline and combative awareness. The modern business world has even attempted to appropriate samurai theory, both as a method of stress control and of improving performance. The age of the samurai is finished, but it is clear that history will not let them go for some time yet.

CHAPTER TWO

DWELLINGS AND DAILY LIFE

Samurai were not a homogenous class of people. Although they had a definite rank within the scheme of feudal Japan, they also had diversity among their members. At one extreme were samurai of great wealth and standing, including the *daimyō* themselves, rulers in their own right. Alternatively, there were samurai who limped by financially, with few retainers and only small holdings of land, which they might even personally tend. The differences that ran through the samurai naturally affected their day-to-day experience of life, from what they did for work to the intensity with which they trained. There was still much that united them, however, as the essential simplicity of Japanese martial philosophy went a long way to preventing unwarranted ostentation. To understand their quotidian lives, however, we first need to see where they lived.

◄ *A daimyō and samurai gather outside Edo, c. 1600, awaiting a formal audience with the local ruler. (Granger Historical Picture Archive/Alamy)*

DWELLINGS

The samurai tended to live in and around their *daimyō*'s castle or mansion. Although the castle itself would project a very visible power and grandeur, with both military and administrative functions, domestic dwellings tended towards a more humble and plain style, steering away from ostentatious displays of wealth.

The focal point for the samurai was the *daimyō*'s castle, from which the lord of the region projected his power and ruled his kingdom, albeit with a constant nod to central government. To Western eyes, Japanese castles are strikingly different to the dour but impressive stone bulwarks built across Europe in the medieval and Renaissance periods. Surviving Japanese castles, such as the great Himeji Castle in Hyogo Prefecture and Nagoya Castle in central Japan, are ornate and decorative, places that as much evoke peaceful contemplation as they projected defensive muscle.

CASTLES

The Japanese castles of the early medieval period were purely wooden affairs, typically comprising stockades, palisades, wooden towers, walkways and gateways of varying sophistication. Placed high on natural features such as mountains and hilltops, these were known as *yamajiro* (mountain castle) and *hirayamajiro* (hilltop castle), while on the plains they were called *hirajiro* (plains castle). In all cases, as much as possible, the castle's structures and defensive arrangements were fully integrated into the landscape. The *yamajiro*'s architects would take advantage of natural slopes,

▲ *Himeji Castle in Hyōgo Prefecture, Japan. The castle was built in the 14th century, although remodelled by subsequent rulers. (Bernard Gagnon/CC)*

▼ *Formerly a country villa for the Fujiwara clan, the Byōdō-in in Uji, Kyoto Prefecture, became a Buddhist temple in 1054. The Phoenix Hall seen here is the only original part; the rest was burned down during war in 1336. (Oilstreet/GFDL)*

▲ *People swarm across the Nihonbashi bridge in Edo. The view up towards Mount Fuji shows a variety of domestic dwellings, as well as the castle. (PD-Art)*

rocky outcrops, hunters' tracks between high points, woodland and other features, working with these to constrain possible attack routes and develop fields of fire for archers and musketmen. For the *hirajiro*, which did not have any advantages of elevation, particular use was made of lakes, rivers, streams and flooded ground, again controlling the ways in which an enemy could direct his attack. Note also that a *daimyō* might have a principal castle plus a number of satellite castles, extending his authority out from the centre of government across the wider region, each castle being managed by one of his senior retainers.

Sengoku *yamajiro*

During the Sengoku *jidai*, the build priorities of the *yamajiro*-type castles underwent a significant change, as the nature of the threat began to shift from relatively uncoordinated assaults by minor forces to major sieges and onslaughts by large and organised land armies. One of the first shifts was the more constructive (literally) use of the landscape in castle fabrication. In what is termed the Sengoku *yamajiro*, hillsides were substantially flattened, their slopes steepened and contoured, often purged of natural cover, creating complexes of semi-conical hill forts, the baileys providing mutually supporting fields of fire. A fine example of the Sengoku *yamajiro* is that of Shigisan Castle, atop Mount Shigi, on the border of Japan's Kawachi and Yamato Provinces. Shigisan was in use between 1536 and 1577, and rose to become the

▶ *A close-up of roof details of Himeji Castle. The main materials used to build the castle were wood, stone and plaster. The circular panels here, dotted evenly along the roof edge, bear family crests. (Terimma/ Shutterstock)*

▲ *Tottori Castle in Inaba Province is a good example of a* yamajiro *(mountain castle), with natural features providing much of the physical defences. (663highland/GFDL)*

governing seat of the *daimyō* of Yamato Province. It presented its defiance through multiple earthen bastions carved from the mountain, of increasing elevations. Ditches around the bases of the bastions were often bisected by cut sections, to form a difficult series of boxlike traps for attacking armies. Gullies were sliced into the mountain slopes to form ready tracks for rolling boulders downhill. The wooden palisade edging each bastion had multiple arrow slits, cut at regular intervals, from which archers could deliver accurate fire. Despite the strengths of the site, however, it didn't stop the castle eventually falling to a siege by Oda Nobunaga in 1577, after which the location was abandoned.

Stone bases and keeps

Cannon artillery did not feature with the same level of distribution in Japanese warfare as it did in Europe. Yet with the advent of gunpowder weapons, from the late 1500s we see Japanese castles transformed with a more pivotal use of stone in the construction. The most substantive shift was seen in a new generation of castles on massive sloped bases, created with monumental, shaped blocks of stone layered on top of natural slopes, thereby creating an immensely thick base slab amply designed both to deflect and 'soak up' incoming gunpowder missiles. At the same time, we witness the use of stone to produce taller and stronger keeps, some up to seven stories high, as focal points for administration, storage and final defence. (Note that often the numbers of floors inside did not correspond with the apparent number of floors viewed from the outside, this arrangement being a deliberate act of defensive disorientation.) The construction of the keep was solid: hefty stone walls, arrow slits, resilient and spiked wooden doors, sally ports and machicolations from which to drop lethal missiles on attackers below. The governmental functions of the keeps were reflected in the ornate style of roof architecture, with tiled roofs and wooden gables of regal grandeur. Aesthetically impressive surviving, or at least reconstructed, examples include keeps at Himeji Castle in the Hyōgo Prefecture or Fushimi Momoyama Castle in Kyoto. Multiple keeps and stone towers, along with complex arrangements of bridges, gates, gatehouses and outer walls – often leading an enemy unknowingly into a killing zone – ensured that castles would not be an easy prospect to capture, regardless of the enemy's ingenuity.

The internal layout of a Japanese fortification was based upon a series of courtyards, baileys or enclosed areas, called

◄ *Despite its highly ornate appearance, Himeji Castle was very defendable. Even today, some 1,000 defensive musket or bow loopholes exist in the walls. (Niko Kitsakis/CC-BY-SA-4.0)*

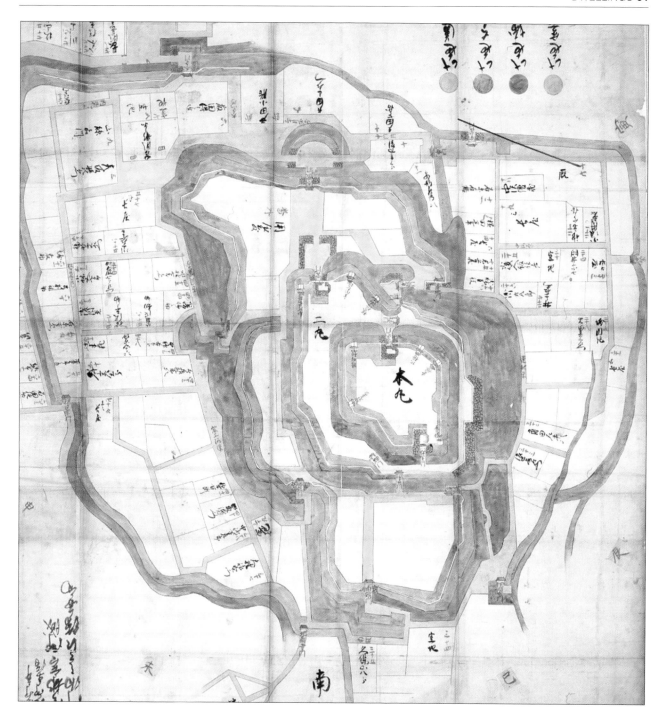

▲ *A map of Utsunomiya Castle, Tochigi, Japan, shows how
waterworks could be built into the concentric rings of
defences. (CC-PD-Mark)*

kurawa. The central *kurawa* was the *hon maru*, and it was
here that the *daimyō* had his keep and, to one side, his
yashiki mansion, where he lived along with family and some of
his most influential samurai retainers. (During the reign of
Tokugawa Ieyasu, the families of *daimyō* were compelled to
live in Edo, effectively as hostages of the shogunate.) Samurai
would also have their own *yashiki* or dwellings outside the
hon maru, both in the castle area and the castle town, these

ranging in stature from multi-room complexes with large
grounds down to single-room affairs, depending on the
samurai's wealth and influence.

SAMURAI HOMES

Regardless of the scale, however, the samurai *yashiki* had a
common style. The whole building occupied a single floor,
with wood framing and panelling, sometimes with simple but
elegant carving, forming the rooms and corridors within.
Room dividers and both inner and outer walls were provided
by *shōji*, the sliding paper screens that traditionally define
Japanese architecture, which generated a serene interplay of

▲ *A modern, but utterly timeless, image of classic Japanese landscaping, both water and land providing spaces for contemplation. (Ivanoff~commonswiki/GFDL)*

light and shade in the interior. The floors were made from polished wood, covered with *tatami* (rice straw) mats. Decoration, with the possible exception of the *daimyō*'s *yashiki*, was largely restrained and calming – the occasional painted scroll; a delicate vase stood on a small table; a flower arrangement; a bonsai tree. These features would be given their own space in a dedicated artistic alcove known as a *tokonoma*. In Japanese etiquette, the most important guest in a room would be seated with his back to the *tokonoma*, to avoid the impression of showing off – modesty was a respected character trait.

Furniture

There would also be very little in the way of furniture in the room, not least because Japanese people of this era sat on the floor, not chairs. Typical elements might include a low desk or a stand for a lamp, and a sword rack in a samurai residence.[3] For heating, there was an absence of the piped hot water seen in some other cultures of this era; traditional Japanese heating would consist of an open fire or a brazier of hot charcoal positioned in the centre of the room. Bedrooms were similarly spartan; the bed and bedding would be kept in discreet cupboards and only brought out at night prior to sleep time. Functional facilities such as the bathhouse (steaming-hot baths were a samurai favourite), kitchens and toilets were generally kept in separate buildings outside the *yashiki*. Historian Stephen Turnbull notes that because toilet facilities were a place were the samurai would truly be alone, they would often be heavily guarded, as they made perfect locations in which out-of-sight assassinations could occur.[4]

Nature

The samurai warrior, like all Japanese citizens, exhibited a fine appreciation of nature. This was more than just an acknowledgement of fresh air and beauty: in traditional Japanese culture, nature represents balance and order, a harmonious natural world reflecting the ideal state of the soul. Nature was also the habitation of various *kami* (spirits). Fields, streams, trees, mountains – all were interlaced with ancestral or natural ghosts. With this in mind, the outer *shōji* of the *yashiki* would ideally slide back to reveal gardens and natural

◄ *A serene* tokonoma *alcove, showing some of the typical decorative items that would be displayed there. (663highland/GFDL)*

► *A chestnut orchard in the main courtyard of Nishikawa Castle. The mounds are actually grassed-over defensive ramparts. (Boneyard90/CC-BY-SA-3.0)*

◤ *A spacious room, of classic Japanese style with* shōji *paper screens, inside Takamatsu Castle, Kagawa Prefecture, Japan. (Fg2/PD)*

features, the exterior world becoming part of the interior peace. The *shōji* also meant that during Japan's hot summer months the airflow could be directed around the house to keep it as cool as possible.

Fire prevention

The downside to the design of the Japanese residence, one exploited to most hideous effect by the US Army Air Forces during the strategic bombing campaign against Japan in 1944–45, was its vulnerability to fire, both accidental and intentional. The '21 Articles' of Hōjō Sōun (1432–1519), a self-made *daimyō* with a life expressed in both war and diplomacy, are an excellent record of the behaviours and etiquette that should underpin the samurai's daily life. Rule 20 contains several dictums about the samurai's responsibility for fire prevention, making sure that fires are properly controlled or extinguished, and that potential fire hazards and flammable materials are diligently cleared away and stored by servants. A watchful samurai would also be careful to ensure that potential access points for enemy arsonists, such as holes dug under fences by wild animals, were filled in and compacted. The rules also (Rule 19) stated that any residence or castle gates should be closed at 6.00pm, and only opened again briefly to let recognised people in or out. Leaving the gates open after this time, the rules made clear, would invite bad things to happen.

▼ *The room here is part of the Shokin-tei tea pavilion in the Katsura Rikyu Imperial Villa. 'Shokin' refers to the sound of a* koto *(Japanese harp). (Raphael Azevedo Franca/PD)*

EVERYDAY DRESS

Samurai warriors were not issued with uniforms but were expected to follow certain rules in what they wore, on and off the battlefield. Simplicity, cleanliness and a lack of affectation were the guiding principles behind the samurai's codes of everyday dress. Ostentation was discouraged, regarded as a sign of boastful character and a lack of humility.

LOINCLOTH

The main undergarment was a *fundoshi* (loincloth), tied in various ways. At its simplest, the loincloth consisted of just a cotton or linen wrap, twisted around the hips, the excess fabric then brought up between the legs and tucked into a cloth belt. A variation featured a cloth loop that attached to the front of the loincloth, with the other end of the loop hung around the neck. Samurai might also wear *tabi* (socks), made from white cloth and with the big toe separated from the other toes, to make it more convenient to wear sandals.

FOOTWEAR

For footwear, the standard options were *waraji* (sandals) or *geta* (clogs), the former made from woven materials such as straw, hemp, plant fibres and cotton, the latter made from wood. In some early artworks, we also see warriors wearing leather boots trimmed with bearskin, known as *kegutsu* or *tsuranuki*, although by the 16th century these had become somewhat rare, and classed as archaic. Samurai might also be seen in short leather riding boots, *kutsu*.

▼ *A close-up of the traditional* waraji *straw sandals. Note how the toes overlap the front slightly; this was an intentional part of the design. (C.Reviver/GFDL)*

KIMONO

The core outer garment worn by the samurai was the kimono, typically made of silk but with budget varieties of cotton or hemp. The samurai would have two weights of kimono: a light one for spring and summer and a heavy one for autumn and winter, changing out of the latter into the former in early May. The early kimonos were one-piece affairs, but from the 12th century a two-piece version known as the *hitatare* – featuring a long-sleeved jacket, and *hakama* trouser-skirt – gradually became standard samurai clothing. For formal dress during the Edo period, the *kamishimo* gave more authority, and featured the wide *hakama* trousers plus the *kataginu*, a sleeveless jacket or vest with particularly wide shoulders, worn over the kimono jacket. For travelling or in bad weather, the *kataginu* could be replaced by a long-sleeved and looser coat known as *haori*. Note that if the samurai was in an informal setting, however, he might replace his trousers with tighter *kobakama* breeches.

▼ *This portrait of a* daimyō *shows him wearing a* kataginu *formal outer jacket, with pointed shoulders. (CC-PD-Mark)*

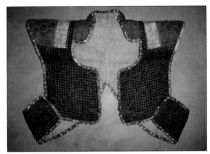

◄ *Far left: A* manju no wa *armored vest, appearing as regular clothing. Left: Another* manju no wa, *with mail and armour plates sewn onto cloth. (Both images Samuraiantiqueworld/CC-BY-SA-3.0)*

▼ *A side view of the humble wooden* geta *clogs. (Haragayato/GFDL)*

WAIST SASH

An important piece of clothing for the samurai was the waist sash (*obi*) that was wrapped around his *hakama*, for it was into this sash that he inserted either one or two swords, worn on his left side. If the samurai was indoors in an informal domestic setting, he might commonly just wear the short sword, while outside or in formal surroundings both blades might be worn, with the long sword sometimes hung from cords rather than inserted straight through the *obi*. Other items that might be tucked into the *obi* included sheets of soft paper that would act as tissues, and possibly a war fan (see Chapter 5).

SUMMARY OF HŌJŌ SŌUN'S 21 ARTICLES

1. Above all, believe in Buddha and the gods.
2. Rise early in the morning. If you get up late, you will neglect your duties and your servants will become slovenly. This will bring the displeasure of your lord.
3. Go to bed and sleep in a decent time, before 8pm, and rise between 3am and 5am. Do not stay up late engaged in profligate conversation.
4. When you wake in the morning, give instructions to your servants for cleaning the property. Wash yourself decorously, without too much throat-clearing or using up too much water.
5. Show your character through your acts. Be simple and straightforward, have respect for those above you and kindness to those below you. Be upright in nature, and you will enjoy the protection of heaven.
6. As for swords and clothes, don't be ostentatious in manner to impress others, for you will invite ridicule. Be plain in dress.
7. Arrange your hair as soon as you rise, and do not let others see you in a slovenly state, even if you are ill.
8. When you go to visit your lord, do not rush in but first observe those in the anteroom and adjust your appearance accordingly. Don't embarrass yourself.
9. Be respectful to your lord, bowing and replying appropriately. Report your business truthfully and without boasting.
10. Do not become involved with gossip and those who spread rumours. If you do, you will eventually lose your reputation with those who matter.
11. Do not let yourself become involved with too many matters. Let events evolve naturally.
12. Read books, but do not let people see you reading – hide the book in your clothing. In your spare time, always practise writing, so you don't forget the characters.
13. Be polite and respectful to senior retainers, showing courtesy as you walk past them.
14. Tell the truth at all times. If you lie, you will eventually be discovered and disgraced.
15. You should study poetry and avoid being boorish or uncultured. Your character is reflected in your words.
16. In your off-duty hours, practise the skills of horse-riding.
17. Make friends with people of quality, such as those who read books and practise penmanship. Do not be friends with those with fritter their time away, or who are wilfully ignorant.
18. When you go home to your dwelling in your off-duty hours, inspect the structure to ensure that it is in good repair. Watch your servants constantly, to make sure that they do not perform stupid actions.
19. In the evening, at 6.00pm, order the gateway to be closed, only opening it again when people come in or out. Don't leave it open permanently – this will invite bad events.
20. In the evening, inspect all the fires in the kitchens and living quarters. Encourage everyone to be vigilant for fire, and make sure that fire hazards, such as loose clothes, are tidied away.
21. Practise the arts of peace with the left hand and the arts of war with the right hand. It is important to master both.

GROOMING

In a sort of 'cleanliness next to godliness' spirit, the samurai encouraged a high standard of grooming. Being clean and presentable was an outward display of inward discipline, and also a visible demonstration of respect for others. Hōjō Sōun's 21 articles have several points that related specifically to cleanliness and the acts of washing or preparing hair.

On waking in the morning, samurai were expected to rise and wash immediately. Sōun said that during the samurai's morning toilet he should perform the action 'stooping under heaven and stepping cautiously on the Earth', repeating a common saying that advocated going about one's business quietly and unobtrusively.

HAIRSTYLES

Hair was given special attention. The classic samurai hairstyle was the *sakayaki*, with the forehead and centre of the head closely shaved in a semi-circular pattern, while the remaining hair in the centre of the head, worn long, was folded into a queue and topknot known as a *chonmage*. This hairstyle was reputedly developed to prevent sweating and

overheating when the samurai was wearing a helmet in battle. Hōjō Sōun recommended that the hair be combed and presented diligently shortly after waking, to put on a presentable appearance for the world. Dishevelled hair was sometimes associated with the *ronin*, the masterless and occasionally dissolute samurai who wandered Japan looking for gainful employment, or trouble. In battle, however, the samurai hair was often allowed to hang loose, kept off the face with a simple *hachimaki* (headband), hence the samurai featured in battle pictures often have a rather wild and ferocious appearance.

Samurai policy on facial hair was variable. Apart from during the early years of the Edo period, full beards were not common or recommended, the samurai shaving off or,

▼ An actress playing the 12th-century female samurai warrior Tomoe Gozen; note the family crest on the outer garments. (Toyokuni Utagawa I/CC-PD-Mark)

▼ This portrait of Tokugawa Ieyasu shows him with the classic *chonmage* topknot, the hair shaved closely on the forehead and sides. (KanōTannyū/PD)

▲ *The samurai topknot, well illustrated in this 19th-century photograph, could be flattened forward or backwards on the head. (Capital Collections/CC-PD-Mark)*

for the stoic, pulling out whiskers with tweezers. Indeed, body hair in general was somewhat frowned upon. Eyebrows, for example, might be shaved off completely and redrawn on the face, higher up on the forehead to give a distinguished appearance. Moustaches would occasionally be seen, however.

THE IMPORTANCE OF APPEARANCE

A reputable samurai was diligent in his standards of grooming, both on and off the battlefield. This was not just a matter of keeping up standards. The *Hagakure*, that great work of samurai guidance written by Yamamoto Tsunetomo, makes explicit that a well-cultivated outer appearance projected a samurai's reputation both to friends and enemies, even beyond his death in battle:

> Although it seems that taking special care of one's appearance is similar to showiness, it is nothing akin to elegance. Even if you are aware that you may be struck down today and are firmly resolved to an inevitable death, if you are slain with an unseemly appearance, you will show your lack of previous resolve, will be despised by your enemy, and will appear unclean. For this reason it is said that both old and young should take care of their appearance.[5]

Tsunetomo's recommendation to always look one's best, even in the face of imminent death, may appear as extreme to modern audiences. Yet viewed in a holistic context of Japanese notions of spiritual and reputational afterlife, they are perfectly understandable. In many ways, the high standards of grooming, as with many samurai cultural practices, can be likened to St Augustine's 5th-century definition of a sacrament – 'an outward and visible sign of an inward and invisible grace.'

► Waraji *sandals worn by monks are hung up off the floor. Note that there was no standard configuration of strap. (CC-BY-3.0)*

FOOD

Food went beyond matters of simple nutrition for the samurai. In fact, that staple of Japanese diet – rice – was fundmentally bound up with the wealth and status of the person who ate it; the more rice one had, the greater was your evident affluence. Yet ultimately the Japanese diet was more a matter of simplicity rather than ostentation.

While rice was the foundation of most meals, the Japanese table was actually one of nutritious diversity. Modern dieticians have recognised that the traditional Japanese diet, being heavily skewed towards the consumption of fruit and vegetables, was beneficial to health and vitality.

RICE

Japan was truly a rice-based nation and economy, with little importation of foreign foodstuffs. The consequences of failure in the rice harvest were dramatic and sometimes appalling. For instance, during the grievous Kyōhō famine of 1732, when the rice harvest collapsed to 10 per cent of its normal levels because of insect infestation and bad weather

(barley and wheat were also hard hit), famine ensued, with a mortality rate of 20 per cent among some regional populations.

The importance of rice was forever in the minds of the farmers who toiled the rice fields. Not that they would enjoy all the benefits of their crop; each autumn, the rice harvest was taxed to the tune of 40–60 per cent by the local *daimyō* and castle lords, the rice then becoming a literal form of salary for paying samurai and other individuals. Many farmers would grow millet as well as their rice crop, and eat the millet as their primary diet. Indeed, farmers would often cultivate secret fields to avoid both taxation and the very real possibility of their own families going hungry during the lean months. Occasionally, the local *daimyō* might arrange field hunts for such crops, punitively gathering the farmers' back-up foods.

The core measure of rice was the *koku*, which measured out at about 120 litres; this was the amount deemed fit to feed one man for a whole year. The samurai was paid in *koku* according to his status and household, and those samurai of lower ranks might receive less than one *koku* per year, having to make up the shortfall from his own enterprise and resources.

In terms of the rice menu, most samurai ate husked rice, the polished rice with which we are most familiar today being a luxury item reserved largely for the wealthiest in society. To stretch the rice supplies further, rice portions might also be

◄ *A woman carries rice cakes on a tray, the rest of the meal wrapped in a decorative cloth. The scythe on her back is for cutting rice stalks. (Walters Art Museum / PD-Art)*

▼ *Glutinous rice is pounded for making into rice cakes in the traditional way. Rice cakes were a good durable campaign food. (katorisi/GFDL)*

▲ *Three reclining samurai listen to a courtesan play the three-stringed* shamisen, as a kamuro *(courtesan in training) carries in a tray of food. (Florilegius/Alamy)*

▲ *This 19th-century print depicts a bowl of seaweed together with a range of seaweed-related foods. (Metropolitan Museum of Art/CC-PD-Mark)*

mixed with millet or wheat. Given its ubiquity, and to stave off potential dietary boredom, the rice could be prepared in a number of ways. The physical method of cooking was often boiling, although factors such as the ratio of water to rice, the liquid in which the rice was boiled, and the length of time for which the rice was cooked could vary the taste and texture quite considerably. End results ranged from defined and relatively firm individual grains through to a mass of rice reduced to the consistency of a soup, or allowed to cool and formed into convenient cakes. Steaming and baking were also typical. Rice would often be mixed with a variety of vegetables and fruits; one common favourite was a fruit rice cake sweetened with honey, often served wrapped in a large leaf by street vendors. A particularly popular type of rice cake was called *mochi*, which was made from rice flour or a mixture of rice and wheat flour.

When thinking about the essential simplicity of many of the rice dishes, we should remind ourselves that in formal meals, culinary ostentation was often frowned upon. In the great exposition of the Kamakura shogunate, *Azuma Kagami* ('Mirror of the East'), compiled in 52 chapters from 1266, a writer recounts how the first shogun – the great Minamoto no Yoritomo – provided a New Year banquet for his nobles and samurai consisting of nothing more than a discrete bowl of rice and a cup of sake.

FRUIT AND VEGETABLES
Typical foods included potatoes, radishes (of nine different types), cucumbers, yams, burdock, aubergines, mushrooms, varieties of spinach, plums, apples, oranges and apricots. Sources of non-meat protein were beans, soy bean curd (tofu) and assorted nuts, especially chestnuts. Soya beans were a foundational flavour in the Japanese diet, in the form of soy sauce and miso (fermented soy bean paste). The Japanese also gathered a rich harvest from coastal areas: seaweed was another source of protein-rich food, and

depending on the type (there were seven common edible varieties) it could be eaten either as a principal ingredient or cut and crumbled up into the rice or a soup to impart an additional flavour and nutrition. Nor was deficiency of fats a problem, as many of the dishes were cooked heavily in oil, which, combined with the fats from nuts, meant that a well-fed samurai would have plenty of flesh on his bones.

MEAT AND SEAFOOD
The largely vegetarian philosophy of Buddhism meant that meat eating was theoretically limited during the age of the samurai, although this general restriction was largely lifted from the time of the Meiji Restoration. Yet even before the 19th century, a meat-free diet was more a background aspiration than dietary reality for most of the samurai. Part of the reason for this was the samurai enthusiasm for bow or spear hunting, the most popular prey being wild boar, bears (roasted bear paws were something of a delicacy), deer, geese, badger and rabbit. Despite this, red meat was still something of a rarity and luxury. Seafood, by contrast, provided a veritable banquet of flavours for the Japanese table, the extensive waters around the Japanese coast, plus inland rivers, providing all manner of food for rich and poor alike. Popular seafood included abalone, mussels, shrimp, clams, octopus, jellyfish, squid, trout, tuna, mackerel, sea bream, bonito and whale meat. Much of the fish (or meat) caught would be salted or smoked for preservation, meaning that protein would remain available even during the leaner winter months.

DINING ETIQUETTE
Whatever the meal, it would always be served with an appropriate and decorous etiquette, a high sense of civility, peaceful, simple and clean surroundings (hygiene was always a priority in Japanese cuisine's preparation and serving) and the best china and eating implements available.

DRINK

During the medieval and Renaissance period, finding uncontaminated water that was safe to drink was difficult in built-up areas, and diseases such as cholera and dysentery were common. Japan was no different, and like other cultures, brewed or distilled alcohol, and drinks made from boiled water were at the forefront of fluid intake.

▲ *This sake is being served in* ochoko, *small cylindrical cups, one of several traditional options for presenting the drink. (Shaiith/Shutterstock)*

SAKE

In Japan, the alcohol element took the form of sake, made from fermented polished rice. Depending on the type of sake, it was served at various temperatures, but was most commonly warmed in a special ceramic flask (*tokkuri*) before being served in small porcelain cups known as *sakazuki* or a *masu* wooden box cup. At the meal, it was regarded as improper for a person to pour his own sake; others should do it for him.

Sake is an alcoholic drink of robust strength, varying from about 9–20% ABV, so an unrestrained samurai could quickly find himself inebriated. Socially, this was not too much of a problem, which was surprising given the general level of restraint and modesty in samurai society. In fact, remaining stoically sober while the rest of the company hit the bottle hard was actually seen as being impolite and judgemental. Although being drunk left the samurai vulnerable to slips of the tongue or lapses in social grace, the presence of drink gave much leeway, and a temporary drop in standards was often forgiven after the event.

TEA

The other pillar of Japanese fluid intake was green tea. Tea drinking was introduced from China in the 12th–14th centuries, at first in a monastic context (it was seen as a way to keep monks awake during their long contemplative duties), but quickly spreading out to the wider population. A pivotal figure in this context was the Zen monk Dai-o (1236–1308), who brought with him from China knowledge of a specific tea ceremony performed in the Chinese monasteries. The ceremony was refined by successive generations of monks until, in the 15th century, a demonstration of the ceremony to the shogun Ashikaga Yoshimasa led to the *cha no yu* ('the Way of Tea') becoming part of wider Japanese society, not just among the religious orders. At first, the tea ceremony was largely confined to the nobility, with visible displays of wealth in the tea-making utensils and setting. Yet in the 16th century, Sen no Rikyū (1522–91), a merchant and tea master for both Oda Nobunaga and Toyotomi Hideyoshi, developed what became known as the *wabi-cha* style of tea ceremony, noted for its simplicity, aesthetic restraint and the humility of its setting. Utensils became simple and practical, meaning that the tea ceremony could be performed by people of all sectors

◄ *Replica golden tea utensils from the Golden Tea Room (a portable gilded tea room of the 16th century), exhibited in the Kyoto City Archaeological Museum. (GFDL)*

TEA CEREMONY

The tea ceremony was subject to variations in practice and timing, but most samurai would have been familiar with the essential elements that brought together the 'Way of Tea'. Responding to an invitation, the samurai would arrive at the *chashitsu* in good time, place their swords on a rack outside, take off their footwear, then enter through the *nijiriguchi*. Once inside, the warriors would take a few quiet moments to appreciate the art or display in the *tokonoma*, before seating themselves around a small hearth in the centre of the room. At this point, the tea master would arrive. This individual was typically a high-ranking samurai, or could be the *daimyō* himself. Upon his entering the room, there would be some gentle conversation, usually a reflection upon the art within the *tokonoma*. Throughout the ceremony, however, the guests and tea master would avoid garrulous conversation, keeping the focus on the events inside the room and avoiding unnecessary distractions.

Next would follow a light but refined meal, served with bowls of warm sake, the meal presented in fine crockery. Once the food had been finished, the samurai would often leave the room while the host prepared the space for the tea ceremony itself, sometimes switching around the decoration in the *tokonoma* (such as replacing a scroll with a flower in a vase). The guests would return to the room, and water was boiled in an iron kettle, while the cups and other utensils were cleaned.

Throughout the ceremony, two specific types of tea were served, of different consistencies: *koicha* (thick tea) and *usucha* (thin tea), the former served first. *Koicha* was also drunk communally from the same bowl, whereas *usucha* was given to the attendants in individual bowls. The boiled water was poured on to the green tea in a special bowl, frothed with a bamboo whisk to give the drink additional texture, and then served.

All of this might sound particularly undemanding, yet the host aimed to move fluidly through every step, with economy and beauty of physical action. The process was akin to that of a martial artist running through a prearranged series of *kata* movements, practised to the extent that they could be performed almost unconsciously.

▼ *An example of the tea ceremony in action, the server demonstrating physical grace as much as a knowledge of the ritual. (Kanō Osanobu/PD-Art)*

of society. The tea room itself – the *chashitsu* – also became humble: a small room (ideally smaller than 4.5 *tatami* in area) accessed by a door known as a *nijiriguchi*, so small that the guests could only enter by stooping or even crawling – a very visible demonstration of humility and equality among the samurai warriors. The samurai would also have to leave their swords outside the tea house; inside, the only weapons the samurai possessed were manners and a keen understanding of the etiquette of the event.

Philosophically, the tea ceremony was anchored in Zen Buddhism, the notion of 'doing without doing', both host and guests clearing their minds of external considerations to appreciate each moment of the simplest of activities. Yet the *chashitsu* could be the location for far more worldly thoughts: the guests might use the ceremony to plot and scheme against those outside, swap intelligence or gossip, forge alliances and even attempt assassinations within the ceremony itself, despite this being a spectacular breach of etiquette. For there were always those who actually had little

▼ *The modern tea ceremony is largely the same as that of the samurai age. Note the* chasen *bamboo whisk. (Georges Seguin/GFDL)*

time for the aesthetic or spiritual elements of the tea ceremony. One such character was Katō Kiyomasa (1562–1611), a renowned warrior and *daimyō*. Kiyomasa was a member of a sect that practised Nichiren Buddhism, thus he was not as wedded to the ceremonial elements that underwrote Zen Buddhism at this time. During one tea ceremony, Kiyomasa took a spear secretly into the *chashitsu*, hoping that the host – a political rival – would be totally absorbed in the rites and thus drop his guard and allow Kiyomasa to strike. The opportune moment never came, however, as the host, despite his ceremonial duties, remained 'in the moment' enough to make clear he was aware of the threat. Thus, Kiyomasa kept his spear concealed and the sanctity of the *cha no yu* was preserved.

▲ *The* Meimei-an *tea house was built in 1779 by Lord Matsudaira Harusato, daimyō of the Matsue clan. (663highland/GFDL)*

Conversely, one legend concerning Kiyomasa shows that he was not entirely disdainful of the value of the tea ceremony. The story goes that while some of his servants were cleaning the *chashitsu* for a ceremony the following day, one of them dropped Kiyomasa's favourite tea bowl, a piece of exquisite quality and refinement. When Kiyomasa discovered the fact, he snapped into a violent rage, and demanded to know who was to blame. The pace of his anger only accelerated when the servants refused to give up the culprit. At first they stayed silent, but then one of the youths – a mere boy of 14 years called Katō Heizaburo – spoke up, saying that they believed Kiyomasa might condemn the guilty party to death by *seppuku*. Kiyomasa bristled, saying that they were cowards for not facing their own possible deaths, but Heizaburo stood

firm, countering that they were not afraid to die, but that ultimately their service in defence of their lord and his realm would be worth far more than the loss of the bowl. Kiyomasa paused and heard the logic in Heizaburo's argument, eventually conceding that all the pages could be trusted and never mentioning the tea bowl again. The story is as illustrative of the samurai mindset as it is of the sanctity of the tea ceremony.

▼ *Three actors present a drama of conflict and love, the courtesan (centre) caught between two rival samurai lovers. Japanese threatre began its development in earnest from the 14th century. (World History Archive/Alamy)*

SAMURAI PASTIMES

The samurai attitude towards free time varied according to time, place and leadership. For some, being a samurai was a matter of rigid focus upon martial matters, ignoring the distractions of art and leisure. For others, an investment in cultural pastimes was the signature of a well-rounded samurai warrior.

Across the full spectrum of samurai history, and allowing for many variations of locale and clan, the attitude to what constituted appropriate pastimes for samurai was not homogenous. Speaking generally, there were those *daimyō* who regarded the cultivation of aesthetic and artistic practices as part and parcel of what it meant to be a samurai, the strengthening of the mind not only reflecting the parallel strengthening of the body, but also improving the samurai's skills in practices such as diplomacy and negotiation. This was especially so with the older clans in Japanese society, established during times in which the arts could flourish, and for whom aesthetic sensibility was part of the warrior identity. For newer clans born in war and desperation, however, there was a tendency among some to view artistic activities as unprofitable; all time spent on such indulgences could, in their view, be better directed into martial training or affairs of state. Thus, some *daimyō* issued *kakun* (household rules) that forbade the samurai to play music, write poetry or go to the theatre, insisting on the supremacy of military matters (*bu*) over the celebration of letters (*bun*), the debate between these two foci known as *bunbu ichi*.[6]

▼ *This illustration from the late 15th century is one of a series showing different occupations in Japan. Here we see a musician (left) playing a bamboo flute, entertaining a samurai administrator. (CC-PD-Mark)*

A particularly famous passage regarding *bunbu ichi* comes from the wisdom of the *Hagakure*, in which Tsunetomo ruminates on the Nabeshima clan (to which Tsunetomo belongs) and its partial disdain for the arts:

> The saying 'The arts aid the body', is for samurai of other regions. For samurai of the Nabeshima clan the arts bring ruin to the body. In all cases, the person who practises an art is an artist, not a samurai, and one should have the intention of being called a samurai.[7]

The statement seems clear – art and war do not mix in the serious warrior. Yet the sentence that follows on from this passage injects a note of ambiguity: 'When one has the conviction that even the slightest artful ability is harmful to the samurai, all the arts become useful to him. One should understand this sort of thing.'[8] Unpacking these two sentences is an exercise in ambiguity. There is the sense that the samurai should not regard the arts as part of being a true warrior, yet at the same time there is the implication that ignorance of the arts altogether is a weakness, preventing them becoming 'useful to him'. Certainly, the *Hagakure* does not encourage boorishness and a conscious rejection of learning. At various points, Tsunetomo emphasises that the well-rounded samurai should cultivate speaking properly (oration), write excellent letters and practise calligraphy, not just spend time wielding the sword.

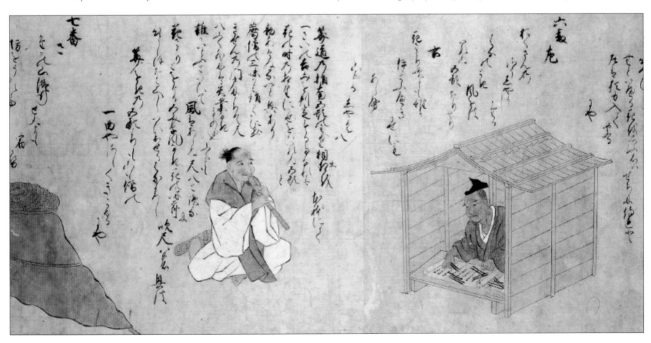

▲ *The* torii *of a Shinto shrine. Those passing through the gateway should regard it as a transition between the daily and the sacred worlds. (Bariston/CC-BY-SA.4.0)*

Tsunetomo elsewhere states that: 'Recently people who call themselves "clever" adorn themselves with superficial wisdom and only deceive others. For this reason they are inferior to dull-witted folk.'[19] Reading the totality of his work, Tsunetomo is not so much opposed to intellectual or artistic activity, but rather to those who pursue such activities in a self-serving way, wishing purely to elevate themselves rather than achieve true humility and wisdom.

WRITTEN ARTS

Much of a samurai's time would be spent directly in the official activities of his position, including administration and practical household affairs, or training in the skills of weapon handling (see Chapter 5). For those clans that did promote artistic endeavours, however, there was a range of possibilities for the conscientious samurai who might have some spare hours on his hands. Calligraphy – or *shodo* ('the way of writing') – was particularly revered, the fluidity and precision required to form the characters with the *fude* (brush) or *sumi* (inkstick) evoking similar desirable skills with a blade.

While calligraphy elevated the form of writing itself, some samurai also embraced content in the form of poetical writing. Traditional Japanese poetry has several different forms,

▶ *A young Japanese samurai on horseback. The two ladies talking confidentially in the window suggests some form of intrigue. (Glasshouse Images/Alamy)*

including *waka*, *tanka* and *haiku*, each form distinguished by metre and length. Another interesting type was the *renga* (linked poem), in which a group of poets produced a collaborative work, the piece evolving as it passed from person to person. Interestingly, the *Hagakure* uses the example of *renga* to illustrate the practice of giving one's entire concentration to something.

Regardless of the form of the poem or manner of its creation, samurai poets could be capable of some exquisite work (allowing for history's bias towards selecting things of value and quality). The following verse comes from the pen of the great Uesugi Kenshin (1530–78), who, like so many Japanese writers, ruminated on the ephemeral nature of life and the enlightened soul's detachment from earthly things:

> Even a life-long prosperity is but one cup of sake;
> A life of forty-nine years is passed in a dream;
> I know not what life is, nor death.
> Year in year out – all but a dream.
> Both Heaven and Hell are left behind;
> I stand in the moonlit dawn,
> Free from clouds of attachment.

The elegance of the writing is striking here, showing that the warrior could indeed cultivate a higher spirit alongside the more brutal aspects of his calling.

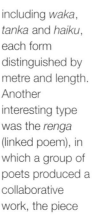

◀ *A thick-ended Japanese calligraphy brush, used for making bold and heavy strokes. In some traditions calligraphy is regarded as akin to a martial art. (Ph0kin/CC-BY-SA-3.0)*

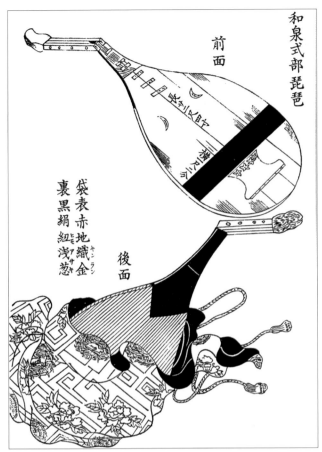

▲ *A 19th-century artwork illustrating a* biwa *short-necked lute. The music of the* biwa *was often used to accompany narrative storytelling. (PD-Japan)*

MUSIC

In addition to poetry, there were many other cultural practices for the high-minded samurai. Playing music was popular, the favoured tools including stringed instruments such as the *biwa*, *gottan*, *kokyū*, *shamisen* or *ichigenkin* or one of a range of haunting wooden flutes, including the *hocchiku*, *nohkan* and *shinobue*.

BOARD GAMES

For those samurai who wanted mental recreation combined with an element of warrior education, he might play *shogi* (lit. 'Game of Generals'), the Japanese equivalent to chess. Like chess, *shogi* had a martial influence behind its gameplay, each move involving longer-term tactical decision-making with an aggressive but careful mindset. Over time, the evolution of the game's rules may have reflected shifts in samurai history. For example, the introduction of the drop rule (whereby a player can keep hold of captured pieces and 'drop' them back into the gameplay again) may have been introduced in the 15th century to mirror the practice of *ronin* switching their loyalties when captured rather than being executed. Regardless of whether this was the case or not, the links between *shogi* and Japan's feudal and warrior past were strong enough for the Supreme Commander of the Allied

Powers (SCAP) government of post-World War II Japan to contemplate banning the game, the Allies debating whether it encouraged prisoner abuse and the darker side of *bushidō* (see Chapter 1).

Another tactical game enjoyed by the population at large, and through which the samurai could demonstrate mental ability, was *go*, introduced into Japan in the 7th century. *Go* was similar to *shogi*, being a two-player game involving each player attempting to capture his opponent's pieces through tactical moves. *Go* rapidly achieved status in imperial circles from the 8th century, spreading out into the wider population during the 13th century. A significant event for its development was the establishment of the Tokugawa shogunate in 1603, for Ieyasu gave *go* an official status, establishing a *godokoro* (minister of *go*) in the Japanese government – a Buddhist monk called Kano Yosaburo – and promoting the development of prestigious *go* schools and national competitions.

THEATRE

Calligraphy, writing poetry, playing music and playing tactical games constituted the more active side of a samurai's leisure options, but there was also passive amusement to be had. Travelling lute players, for example, would visit the samurai castles, providing mood-filled musical renditions of samurai legends, for the entertainment and also implicit education of the listening samurai, the stories illustrating both the glory and the downfall of great men in action. There was also the lure of theatre, performed either at theatre houses or on the premises of the *daimyō* or lord by travelling theatre troupes.

There were three main forms of theatre for the samurai: *noh*, *kabuki* and *ningyo joruri*, the latter also known as *bunraku*. *Noh* theatre involved plays performed by an all-male cast, each character utilising masks, dance and song (a four-man musical crew providing the soundtrack) to re-enact tales from history or legend, often laced with a deep mood of supernaturalism. The characters of the *noh* plays included

▼ *The world's oldest existing* noh *stage at Itsukushima Shrine, Miyajima Island, Hiroshima Prefecture, Japan. (Arcimboldo/ CC-BY-SA-3.0)*

archetypes such as demons, the wise old man, a priest, a monk and a samurai. The drama could unfold over some time, so the weight was periodically alleviated by the performance of comical pieces known as *kyōgen*.

While *noh* theatre had its origins back in the 14th century, *kabuki* arrived somewhat later, the first performances appearing in 1603. *Kabuki* was originally far more populist and expressive than *noh*, featuring larger casts of mixed gender, occasionally raunchy themes, and song and dance. Indeed, *kabuki*'s female-heavy cast apparently blurred the lines between acting and prostitution, and from the late 1620s the shogunate began to clamp down, at first banning females from performing and then, in 1652, prohibiting young men and boys, many of whom also served as prostitutes, from the *kabuki* stage – from now on only mature men could grace the boards. During the later Genroku period (1688–1704), however, *kabuki* became more formalised and stylised, and gradually its status rose, although the shogunate still kept a watchful eye on the theatre companies, and often controlled the locations in which the plays could be performed.

Bunraku was one of the newer forms of traditional Japanese theatre, originating like *kabuki* in the 17th century. It contrasted with both other forms by being puppet theatre, the puppeteers manoeuvring beautifully carved and dressed figures, accompanied to music and chant. Although *bunraku* undoubtedly had a popular audience, it still dealt with typically weighty themes of love, loyalty, war and death.

The level to which the samurai indulged in theatre is unclear. Certainly, we know that the *noh* performers entertained samurai audiences, the moralistic content and dignity of the performances making it acceptable for it to be performed in the loftiest of *daimyō* residences. Yet the samurai's access to and fondness for theatre varied from place and place and from time to time, and much of the life of

▼ *A 19th-century painting depicts a major* kabuki *theatre production. The audience are watching the* Shibaraku, *a short (c. 50-minute) play. (Toyokuni Utagawa III/CC-PD-Mark)*

► *A game of* kemari, *here played at the* Kemari Matsuri *(Kickball Festival) at the Tanzan Shrine in Sakurai, Nara Prefecture. (radBeattie/GFDL)*

local theatre would depend upon the outlook of both the shogunate and the *daimyō*, and of the samurai himself.

KEMARI

An account of samurai pastimes would be incomplete without mentioning *kemari*, a lively physical game that must have provided a welcome break for minds weighed heavily with etiquette and martial responsibilities. For Western audiences, *kemari* is best summed up as a form of ritualistic, non-competitive football, much like the playground pastime of 'keep it up'. The ball is known as a *mari*, and is made from deerskin (the hide is the outer face of the ball) stuffed with barley or sawdust, and the pitch is an area of about 6–7m (20–23ft) squared, called a *kikutsubo*. The extent of the pitch was marked out by trees, either planted permanently (usually a practice of the wealthy) or in portable pots. In traditional *kemari*, four specific types of tree demarcated the border of the pitch: cherry, maple, willow and pine.[10]

The rules of *kemari*, which were established in Japan in the 13th century (although the game had gravitated over from China far earlier than that), basically involved two to eight players working cooperatively to keep the ball in the air, without using their hands or arms at any point. The person who was kicking the ball was called the *mariashi*, every time he kicked the ball he would shout *Ariya!*, eventually passing the ball to the next *mariashi* with the cry of *Ari!* The game has survived to this day, and can still be seen played in traditional clothing at the sites of shrines.

The daily life of the samurai, as we have seen, was largely a world apart from the violence that awaited him on the battlefield. However, especially during Japan's most turbulent years, that violence was an ever-present possibility, and death a daily reality. To cope with such a world, the samurai needed a robust spirituality, the subject of our next chapter.

▲ *Here seen wearing a flowing kimono, Fujiwara no Michinaga (966–1028) was a ruler of the Fujiwara clan. (Kikuchi Yōsai/CC-PD-Mark)*

PROSTITUTION

One of the socially darker 'pastimes' of the samurai was a fondness for prostitutes, of whom there was rarely a lack either around the castle towns or while on campaign. Artistic representation has done much to distort this practice, through its highly poetic and romantic visual depictions of elite courtesans, such as those by masters like Hishikawa Moronobu and Katsukawa Shunshō. Reality could be far more prosaic and sordid.

Brothels were common throughout much of Japanese history, with major concentrations in certain districts, the most famous being the Yoshiwara pleasure district just outside of Tokyo. (Note that this was also the area in which many of Edo's *kabuki* theatres were located.) This area was established during the Edo period, when the Tokugawa shogunate was actually looking to resurrect traditional values when it came to sexual relations. Fearing a moral purge, a brothel owner negotiated with the government to locate his facility within a specific area, which could then be appropriately taxed and controlled by the government. He got his way, and the Yoshiwara district both grew and flourished. By 1642, it has been estimated that there were 942 prostitutes in Yoshiwara; by 1800, some 4,000 prostitutes were working in the district. Other major centres included Shimbara in Kyoto, Maruyama in Nagasaki and Shinmachi in Osaka.

Regardless of where they were based, Japan's prostitutes had a hard existence, which in many cases constituted practical slavery. Many of the women who entered prostitution did so as children, sold to brothels at the age of around seven or eight by poor rural families, desperate for money and survival. Although the contract of this sale was often fixed, typically for around ten years, in reality the female was unlikely to leave the brothel as an adult, having accrued debts that needed to be 'worked off'. At first, they would be used as assistants, performing chores around the brothels, but would eventually be shifted into sex work, their virginity often commanding a high price of sale.

If a child showed particular beauty or grace, then around the age of 11 or 12 she might enter into the ranks of those training to be elite courtesans, destined to serve *daimyō*, lords, samurai and wealthy merchants. Their training instructed them in etiquette and the arts, often to high levels, alongside practices such as performing the tea ceremony and playing various intellectual games, such as *go*. When they eventually emerged into the market, they were therefore well-rounded and socially sophisticated individuals who would be at home among the rich and the powerful.

Courtesans were, however, organised into various ranks, their position influencing their pay, status and working conditions. The lower ranks of courtesan had no say over their customers, while the very top ranks required the samurai to undergo a form of application, which might be rejected by the courtesan herself. Regardless of rank, though, the life of both courtesan and common prostitute was ultimately one of survival amid a brutal world, fending off those who would take their clients while trying to retain the interest of the customers.

CHAPTER THREE

SAMURAI SPIRITUALITY

As the introduction to this book explains, we must be careful about over-spiritualising the profession of the samurai. Much of the modern philosophical framework that we ascribe to samurai warriors comes from times of peace, particularly the relative stability of the Tokugawa shogunate and the diplomatic stability of the Meiji Restoration. It is easy to wax philosophical about the bonds between the spiritual and martial dimensions when it is only likely to be the former that is tested in one's life.

 *The Zenkō-ji Buddhist temple dates back to the 7th century, and was used by Uesugi Kenshin as a base of operations in later Japanese history. (Alamy)*

MEDITATIONS ON DEATH

During the era of Warring States, the samurai existence could genuinely be brutal and short, with violent death being an expected outcome rather than outside possibility. The *Hagakure* urged samurai that they should meditate on their death graphically and earnestly as routine:

> Every day when one's body and mind are at peace, one should meditate upon being ripped apart by arrows, muskets, spears and swords, being carried away by surging waves, being thrown into the midst of the great fire, being struck by lightning, being shaken to death by a great earthquake, falling from a thousand-foot cliff, dying of disease or committing *seppuku* at the death of one's master. And every day without fail one should consider himself as dead.[11]

A bleak message indeed, but one born from realism and experience rather than gratuitous imagination. The art that depicted the deaths of samurai often lingered upon the physical characteristics of violent death as much as the spiritual defiance of the samurai, showing the warrior bleeding and staggering under multiple sword or arrow strikes. Several historical accounts attest to the presence of fear among even the most hardened warriors, or at least provide instructions to guard against it. In the *Heieki Yoho*, a major work of tactical thinking by the 17th-century Natori-ryu military school, the author urges samurai to avoid showing any signs of being startled by battle, as this indicates cowardice. He

further implores that the samurai should not go pale, as the volume of blood in his cheeks indicates his level of courage. No specific recommendation is made about how to avoid this involuntary reaction, but it is clear that the warrior class still needed to morally gird itself for battle.

In this environment, whatever spiritual system was adopted had to help the warrior cope with the uniquely brutal conditions of life. It is for this reason that the study of contemporary Japanese religion is essential to understanding the life and behaviour of the samurai. As we shall see in this chapter, samurai spirituality was formed from an amalgam of sources, ranging from highly organised formal religions through to more organic local traditions.

◄ *A statue of Kōmokuten, the Buddhist guardian deity. The name literally translates as 'Wide Eyed' or 'Expansive Vision'. (CC-PD-Mark)*

► *Samurai armour, as displayed in Tokyo National Museum, instantly conveys the Japanese warrior spirit. (Ian Armstrong/CC-BY-SA-2.0)*

THE RELIGIONS OF JAPAN

To map out the spiritual landscape of the samurai, we need at least a basic grasp of the four faiths that made up the Japanese religious world: Shinto, Taoism, Confucianism and Buddhism. Taken together, and merged with varying degrees of flexibility, the samurai was able to see the world through an amalgam of faith systems perfectly attuned to the reality of his life and surrounding nature.

SHINTO

Shinto is one of the earliest forms of religion in Japan. It is an elusive faith to define in terms of doctrine and practice, as it is largely concerned with the performance of localised traditions and rituals as interactions between the human world and that of the *kami*, the spirits of ancestors or the spiritual characters of natural features, such as rivers, rocks, trees, forests and mountains. A body of priests or shamans acted as intercessors between this world of the spirits and that of the humans, interpreting natural phenomena and performing a mix of rituals to placate the otherworldly beings, gain their blessing or divine their will. Although Shinto had no defining doctrine as such, its theological traditions did have figures in an overarching pantheon. Amaterasu, for example, was classed as the goddess of the sun and the universe, and according to tradition, the emperors of Japan were directly

▼ *The restored western gate of Ki Castle. The castle's name means 'demon castle', referring to the belief that a demon once ruled Kibi Province from the fortress. (Reggaeman/GFDL)*

descended from her godhead. This is not just an interesting political side. Rather, by integrating the emperor into the world of the *kami*, it gave a sense of divine right to his activities – and to his samurai armies – that would have been appreciable throughout the population of Japan.

ANCESTOR WORSHIP

The veneration of the *kami* was also bound up with wider Japanese practices of ancestor worship, which in the syncretic way of Japanese religion was also infused with certain Buddhist rites. When a person died, the worst outcome was that they died as *muenbotoke*, spirits without descendants or family/clan affiliations, or those who had died in a particularly brutal or sudden fashion, and hence remained attached angrily to the world rather than passing over to the next dimension. For the others, thankfully the majority, they now began a long journey to becoming *kami*, a journey that was partly guided from this world by the performance of specified rituals, prayers and ceremonies by their relatives and descendants. The aim was first to separate the spirit from the

▲ *Heike and Genji forces clash on the rocky shore at Ishibashiyama within sight of a moonlit Mount Fuji, in this poetic vision of warfare. (Walters Art Museum/PD)*

◄ *The sacred tree to the right of this picture is a* shinboku, *and is regarded as a place where spirits dwell. It is forbidden to cut or damage such trees. (CC-BY-SA.3.0)*

▼ *The swordsmith Munechika (10th century) is assisted in his art by the presence of a fox spirit. He is forging the blade Ko-Gitsune Maru ('Little Fox'). (Ogata Gekkō/CC-PD-Mark)*

physical world, transforming the deceased into *shirei* (a spirit of the recently dead) over a period of 49 days. Over subsequent decades, the repetition of the rituals moved the spirit to become first a *hotoke* (enlightened one) and finally, after either 33 or 50 years (traditions vary), the spirit would merge into the greater body of family spirits, to become *kami*.

For the *kami*, Shinto rituals and ancestor worship informed his daily life and his practice as a warrior. He would visit Shinto shrines on a regular basis, both offering his respects to his ancestors or performing rituals of purification, personal protection, divination, etc. The shrines themselves would have bestowed a calming effect on troubled minds, typically being places of simple tranquillity and beauty, most easily identified by the *torii* gateway, shaped like the Greek letter *pi*. The samurai's household would also have a *kamidana*, a miniature household altar set on a small cupboard or high shelf, containing various items of veneration and the means of making offerings, the whole acting as a focal point for the worship of family *kami*. The samurai could also connect with the *kami* via *ema*, small wooden plaques on which the worshipper would write his prayers and requests for guidance, depositing the prayer-plaque at a Shinto shrine, where its message would be communicated to the *kami*. Oda Nobunaga made this form of worship in 1560, when he wrote a prayer for victory at the forthcoming Battle of Okehazama and placed it in the great Atsuta Shrine, near modern Nagoya. His wish was granted.

The fact that, through Shinto and other elements of folk religion, the ancestral afterlife played such an important part in the samurai psychology, had a further important implication. The samurai would wish to do nothing in life that would bring shame to him or his family and death. Thus, courage on the battlefield was not just a matter of personal pride, it was also essential if he was to go into the afterlife in the right manner, his life and passing destined to be celebrated by those who would aid in his ascent to *kami*.

◄ *The family crest of the great Tokugawa clan. In many ways, family was the basis for much of the samurai philosophy and organisation. (Lemon-s/ PD-User)*

BATTLEFIELD RITUALS

Shinto rituals of purification might also be performed prior to battle, cleansing the battlefield of spiritual malevolence. Yet we also see shamans employed in even more direct tactical roles. In the *Heieki Yoho*, Masazumi (the author) explains that multiple *gunbaisha* – or 'esoteric tacticians' – are a necessary component of the military headquarters. These were people who would 'read' the spiritual undercurrents of warfare, and would then make recommendations or perform rituals to ensure that good fortune supported the combat endeavours. The list of factors they would consider was extensive, and to modern eyes reads like a mix of battlefield feng shui and age-old divination:

- date
- time
- directions (positive and negative)
- the influence of the season upon military strength
- divination
- luck
- astrology
- inspection of decapitated heads
- ritual arrow shooting
- the appropriate use of war cries
- rituals for donning military equipment
- the use of talismans
- casting spells[12]

The *gunbaisha* need not necessarily have been Shinto priests, although many likely were, but their list of spiritual concerns and tools illustrates just how pervasive the religious factors were in the age of samurai warfare. Shinto priests would also perform rights of purification on the many dead bodies that littered the battlefield after action. Human corpses, and also the biological act of childbirth, were regarded as pollutants under the Shinto faith, and had to be cleansed through ritual before both the dead and the newly born could be handled without contamination.

CONFUCIANISM

Confucianism presents something of a contrast to Shinto, both in its spiritual outlook and also in the political influence it exercised on Japanese society. Like Buddhism and Taoism, Confucianism originated in China in the 6th century BC, and was based on the writings of the personality known in the West as Confucius, more accurately referred to as K'ung. From relatively humble beginnings, K'ung managed to engineer his advance through Chinese society to achieve noble status and high position in government, fulfilling his ambitions through education, an observance of etiquette and diplomacy, and a good character. Given his life path, it is relatively unsurprising that K'ung's teachings (he wrote extensive guidance for his subordinates) would form the basis of a religion that emphasised the rules of propriety and ceremony. In the *Analects*, a collection of K'ung's teachings written approximately 70 years after his death, the 'Master' described decorous relations between people:

> The Master said: 'Respectfulness, without the rules of propriety, becomes laborious bustle; carefulness, without the rules of propriety, becomes timidity; boldness, without the rules of propriety, becomes insubordination; straightforwardness, without the rules of propriety, becomes rudeness. When those who are in high stations perform well all their duties to their relations, the people are aroused to virtue. When old friends are not neglected by them, the people are preserved from inferiority.
> 'Though a man has abilities as admirable as those of the Duke of Chou, yet if he be proud and niggardly, those other things are really not worth being looked at.'[13]

In K'ung's world, correct behaviour and observing of social context were critical to good character. K'ung was also prescriptive about the right relationships between family members and between people and their superiors. The actual spiritual, rather than practical, content of Confucianism is not always clear. Heaven is acknowledged as a definite realm, as is a divine presence, established codes of good and evil, and

▼ *Modern wooden* ema *prayer plaques, the user's prayers written around the image. Horses and chickens are common symbolic images. (Fg2/PD)*

the need for ancestor worship. Yet some have seen in Confucianism an essentially humanistic and rationalistic faith, and it was these qualities that became useful to the Japanese when it reached Japan during the Kamakura period.

Edo Neo-Confucianism, as the Japanese form of the faith has been called, was fostered and encouraged by the Tokugawa shogunate. Its appeal to government was that the secular elements to Confucianism provided a means of political rule that transcended local varieties of religion. Following the Kansei Edict of 1790, Neo-Confucianism of the variety advocated by the Confucian scholar Zhu Xi became the official Confucian philosophy of Japan.

Confucianism's emphasis on correct behaviour, education, rationality and social standards can be seen in many of the philosophical writings of prominent samurai. Miyamoto Musashi's great *The Book of Five Rings*, a seminal work on personal samurai fighting tactics, declares that 'in composing this book, I have not borrowed the old sayings of Buddhism or Confucianism'. Yet it still reflects general propriety, and the value of intelligence, in its lessons. He recommends for anyone wanting to learn about military science:

1. Think of what is right and true.
2. Practise and cultivate the science.
3. Become acquainted with the arts.
4. Know the principles of the crafts.
5. Understand the harm and benefit in everything.
6. Learn to see everything accurately.
7. Become aware of what is not obvious.
8. Be careful even in small matters.
9. Do not do anything useless.[14]

His perspectives on the self-aware character are echoed by Yagyū Munenori (1571–1646), another master of swordsmanship, in his *The Family Traditions on the Art of*

▲ *Kōfuku-ji, a 7th-century Buddhist temple, was variously damaged and destroyed by wars over subsequent centuries of Japanese history. (PD-Self)*

War. Munenori spoke passionately of 'The Great Learning', likening wise education to passing through a gate of understanding. In his opinion, The Great Learning 'speaks of consummating knowledge and perfecting things. Consummating knowledge means knowing the principles of everything that people in the world know. Perfecting things means that when you know the principle of everything thoroughly, then you know everything, can do everything.'[15] Such beliefs underwrote the emphasis for the samurai to cultivate knowledge and artistic sensibility.

Confucianism also had a place on the battlefield, as Natori Masazumi explained in his *Heieki Yoho*. Like the *gunbaisha*, the *jusha* (Confucianists) acted as consultants to the commanding general, in much the same way that they would do for *daimyō* or senior samurai in peacetime life. Often by providing examples of behaviour from ancient history, the *jusha* would attempt to correct

▶ *Kongōrikishi is one of the fierce warrior figures often seen guarding the entrance of Buddhist temples. This figure was originally in Osaka. (Quadell/GFDL)*

▲ *A view of the Usa Jingū Shinto shrine in the city of Usa in Ōita Prefecture. As with many temples, it was periodically damaged by conflict, being burned to the ground in the 16th century. (Dana and LeRoy Bunward/CC-BY-2.0)*

KO AND *CHU*

Two concepts within Confucianism that became central to samurai thinking, and which can help explain some of the extremes of samurai behaviour, are *ko* (filial piety) and *chu* (loyalty). The former referred not only to devotion to parents and grandparents who were alive, but could also extend out to deceased ancestors, and to one's ruler, as head of the clan 'family'. The loyalty most visibly manifested itself in respect for elders or superiors, contributing towards the well-being of the greater group, and the diligent performance of duties. *Chu* reinforced the need for being obedient towards one's rulers, although there was also the requirement upon rulers to be just and sage in their dealings with those they governed. When *ko* and *chu* were maintained, even in times of great turbulence and violence, there was the possibility of some order in the universe.

emotional imbalances in the leader, and bring him to a more rational level of decision-making in the alternative courses of action. They might also perform diplomatic services between the opposing sides, such as assessing letters of reconciliation and appeals for surrender.[16]

BUDDHISM

Of all the religions that migrated into Japan, Buddhism is arguably the one that had the greatest impact on the samurai. The tenets of Zen Buddhism, particularly relating to its mental detachment from material existence and its processes for controlling thought and deed, were ultimately absorbed directly into samurai martial thinking and training, including into the practical techniques of archery and swordsmanship. And yet Buddhism in Japan was as much a political force as a spiritual one, and this reality partly explains

▲ *Kamei Koremi (1824–85) was one of the key officials responsible for separating Buddhism from Shinto rites during political reforms of the Meiji period. (PD)*

▲ *A man wearing full samurai armour, including the ferocious* menpō *face mask, participates in a re-enactment event at the Sannosai Festival. (Photo Japan/Alamy)*

how Zen Buddhism became so connected to the warrior spirit.

Buddhism first came into contact with Japanese culture during the 6th century, via Korean officials who had in turn received Buddhism from China. The tenets of Buddhism depended somewhat on the particular sect or branch, but they revolved around the core philosophy that life was defined by impermanence and suffering, the latter born from human desire yearning for life to be other than what it actually is. Through an ascetic life, and meditative practices, the Buddhist practitioner could eventually understand the true reality of his existence and that of the world beyond, finding enlightenment (*satori*) and freedom from the pain and suffering and rebirth, eventually entering the realm of nirvana.

When it first entered Japan, Buddhism was primarily practised by high-ranking officials in the imperial court, but as it began to fuse itself with Shinto, it spread out into the wider population, and it was officially adopted as the state religion in the early 8th century. By making Buddhism a government-backed religion, the Japanese state could foster the growth of Buddhist beliefs as they saw fit, authorising 'official' Buddhist monks and schools, and controlling the content and extent of preaching, in much the same way as the Catholic Church governed access to religious knowledge during the medieval and Renaissance periods.

During the late Heian period, and the subsequent Kamakura era, state Buddhism fragmented into various sects, particularly True Pure Land, Nichiren and Zen, and these in turn spread throughout a land that was becoming more polarised and violent. By way of consequence, Buddhism became associated with a militant and militaristic expression of religion, despite Buddhism's deep philosophical advocacy of peaceful behaviour. Buddhist temples, under threat from rival sects and conquering warlords, increasingly developed their own private security forces, either through mercenaries or by training the monks themselves in martial techniques. The rise of the 'warrior monk' in Japanese society would be significant for the samurai, as it established spiritual underpinnings to violent practices.

Samurai adoption

Zen Buddhism emerged as the forerunner among the samurai warrior class during the early Kamakura period, the widow of Minamoto Yoritomo – Hōjō Masako – assisting in the establishment of Zen temples in Kyoto. Buddhism quickly caught on among the samurai, who found in much of Zen's teachings a route to achieving spiritual peace even during times of war and likely death. Zen Buddhism, through its meditative practices and its sense of mental transcendence, seemed to offer a way in which the samurai could face death with a passionless sense of detachment – i.e. without fear. Zen practices also developed concentration combined with a lack of self-consciousness, and the resulting deep and instinctive hyper-awareness of the world also hinted at ways of sharpening combative skills. In his teaching of swordsmanship, Yagyū Munenori frequently refers to the sayings and principles of Zen Buddhism to illustrate this point. For example:

The vanguard of the moment is before the appellant has begun to make a move. This first impulse of movement is the energy, feeling, or mood, held back in the chest. The dynamic of the movement is energy, feeling, or mood. To accurately see an opponent's energy, feeling, or mood, and to act accordingly in their presence, is called the vanguard of the moment. This affective action is the specialty of Zen, where it is referred to as the Zen dynamic.[17]

Later in the work, Munenori emphasises the point that 'Attachment is despised in Buddhism', this referring to any sort of temporal mental dependency, including the warrior's fondness for his own existence.

Zen also came to be associated with the practice of archery. Trained under the influence of a Zen master, the samurai archer attempted to purge himself of the preening desire to hit the centre of the target, which resulted in hard and conscious effort, an 'attachment' to the need for accuracy. Instead, the master would try to get the samurai to free himself from this dependency; ironically, in the process of doing so, the samurai's full concentration would flow into the target and his shots would eventually hit precisely the right spot, this moment physically representing the instance of *satori*. In such ways, Buddhism became enmeshed with the warrior identity of the samurai, and would forever carry these associations.

▼ *The powerful Japanese* daimyō *Takeda Katsuyori (1546–82) launches his troops against the castle of Nagashino in 1575. (Rama/CC-PD-Mark)*

▼ *Mythology and history could be intertwined in Japanese lore. Here the 10th-century bureaucrat Fujiwara no Hidesato fights a giant centipede with a bow. (CC-PD-Mark)*

TAOISM

Taoism arrived in Japan from China in the late 7th and early 8th centuries. This particularly esoteric religion did not have the formative effect on samurai mentality as did Buddhism, but some Taoist concepts did have special cultural importance, and fused with elements of the other religions to help shape the samurai outlook.

Understanding Taoism is not easy, as many of its core texts, such as the *Tao Te Ching*, are infused with a rather opaque mysticism. For example, the *Tao Te Ching*, written by Lao Tzu in either the 4th or 6th century BC, begins:

> The Tao that can be expressed is not the eternal Tao;
> The name that can be defined is not the unchanging name.
> Non-existence is called the antecedent of heaven and earth;
> Existence is the mother of all things.
> From external non-existence, therefore, we serenely observe the mysterious beginning of the universe;
> From eternal existence we clearly see the apparent distinctions.[18]

▼ *The* kabuki *stage was an environment in which samurai behaviour was often visualised and explored. (Gift of Mr and Mrs Peter P. Pessutti/Brooklyn Museum)*

▲ *Various forms of helmet crests (*maedate*). Samurai arms and armour were replete with symbolism. (Samuraiantiqueworld/CC-BY-SA-3.0)*

The mysterious and unnameable oneness of the Tao, the force that governs the universe, is the central motif of Taoism, and in many ways was representative of the 'emptiness' the warrior was meant to achieve in battle. By emptying the mind of slow, conscious thought, and responding intuitively to the way the universe unfolded in battle, the warrior would actually have superior reactions, better control of fear, and clarity of mind.

Another principle at the heart of Taoism was the ancient motif of Yin-Yang. Represented most clearly by the famous t'ai chi symbol, Yin-Yang illustrated both the dualism of the world but also how elements of opposing forces were interrelated and connected. The challenge of managing Yin-Yang was essentially to live on the line between the opposing forces, in perfect balance, and it was therefore almost natural that the idea would gravitate into martial arts' philosophy, including the schools of swordsmanship followed by the samurai. Great tactical works, such as *The Book of Five Rings*, are imbued with the idea of using opposing forces to win an encounter. Thus, when the opponent attacks, the swordsman might yield, or when the attacker shows anger, the defender should be at peace. Miyamoto Musashi recommended that a warrior's state of mind should be neither tense nor too relaxed, but perfectly balanced in the middle. It also recommends (admittedly being a bit vague on the specifics) that a small person should know what it is like to be large, and a large person small. The Natori-ryu school explained that there are four basic areas of study in the military schools of the day:

1. strategic thinking
2. situational analysis
3. the study of Yin-Yang
4. practical warrior skills

Taoism is a complex and winding religion, and space does not allow us to dwell on all of its aspects in depth. Suffice to say that the samurai mentality appropriated elements of Taoism as it did many other religious traditions.

DEATH AND LOYALTY

One of the most striking things to confront modern readers about the samurai is their preoccupation with death. To a large degree, death was a conscious accompaniment to every waking moment of the samurai's life. It was both his destiny – even just at a purely biological level – and in many ways his moral obligation, death often being the fulfilment of unswerving loyalty to his master.

The acceptance of death was also written into the religious ritual and doctrines that framed the samurai's world view. Such was particularly the case in reference to Zen Buddhism, with its abiding focus on the impermanence of the physical body and the passing of all things. Tsunetomo said, 'the way of the samurai is found in death'. Understanding what he meant is essential to comprehending not only the very way in which the samurai lived his life, but also for sensing the underpinnings of samurai battlefield tactics. While we can acknowledge that the death-facing perspective of the samurai had philosophical and religious origins, we must be careful not to make it too spiritualised, and thus disconnect death from its very practical and social relevance.

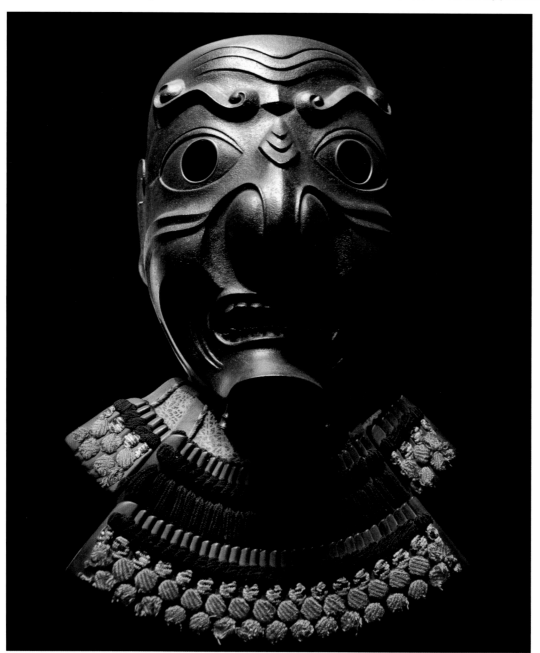

◀ *A full samurai face mask, known as a* sōmen, *was a means both to channel the wearer's aggression plus intimidate the enemy. (Vassil/ CC)*

▶ *General Akashi Gidayu preparing to commit* seppuku *after losing a battle for his master in 1582. (www.japaneseprintauction.com/PD-Art)*

THE WAY OF DEATH

Yamamoto Tsunetomo provides one of the most useful entry points to this discussion at the beginning of the *Hagakure*, in its second verse. The passage is worth quoting at length, as it provides the context for much that is to come:

> The way of the samurai is found in death. When it comes to either/or, there is only the quick choice of death. It is not particularly difficult. Be determined and advance. To say that dying without reaching one's aim is to die a dog's death is the frivolous way of sophisticates. When impressed with the choice of life or death, it is not necessary to gain one's aim.
>
> We all want to live. And in large part we make our logic according to what we like. But not having attained our aim and continuing to live is cowardice. This is a thin dangerous line. To die without gaining one's aim *is* a dog's death and fanaticism. But there is no shame in this. This is the substance of the way of the samurai. If by setting one's heart right every morning and evening, one is able to live as though his body were already dead, he gains freedom in the way. His whole life will be without blame, and he will succeed in his calling.[19]

When reading this passage, what strikes most of us first is the curious logic of accepting death as a way to achieve 'freedom in the way'. In this world, if the samurai does not embrace his

THE LAST TESTAMENT OF TORII MOTOTADA

Torii Mototada (1539–1600) was a renowned samurai who served Tokugawa Ieyasu. Mototada was a most loyal servant, and served in most of Ieyasu's campaigns, being wounded on several occasions. He rose to become the *daimyō* of the fief of Yahagi, Shimōsa Province, being granted 40,000 *koku* (see Chapter 2). In August 1600, Mototada found himself in command of the 2,000-man garrison of Fushimi Castle, which now stood in the way of 40,000 warriors led by Toyotomi Hideyori. Knowing with certainty that the castle would eventually fall, Mototada accepted his fate and wrote a final letter to his son, Tadamasa. In his second paragraph, Mototada explains that retreating in advance of the attack was not his style:

> For myself, I am resolved to make a stand within the castle and to die a quick death. It would not take much trouble to break through a part of their numbers and escape, no matter how many tens of thousands of horsemen approached for the attack or by how many columns we were surrounded. ...By doing so I will show that to abandon a castle that should be defended, or to

value one's life so much as to avoid danger and to show the enemy one's weakness is not within the family traditions of my master Ieyasu.

The devotion to his purpose and end is unswerving. Reminding ourselves of the Confucian value of *chu*, Mototada goes on to explain why those who lack the instinct for loyalty bring both shame on themselves and others:

> Being affected by the avarice for office and rank, or wanting to become a *daimyō* and being eager for such things ... will not one then begin to value his life? And how can a man commit acts of martial valour if he values his life? A man who has been born into the house of a warrior and yet places no loyalty in his heart and thinks only of the fortune of his position will be flattering on the surface and construct schemes in his heart, will forsake righteousness and not reflect on his shame, and will stain the warrior's name of his household to later generations. This is truly regrettable.

ultimate mortal destiny, and lose the dependency that comes from the fear of death, then he will be unable to fight with clarity or vigour. There is something eminently pragmatic about this viewpoint. As we shall see in later chapters, although the samurai warriors did consider ways to take tactical advantage, this was not an era of sophisticated manoeuvre warfare. On the samurai battlefield, what counted above all was to overcome fear, to dismiss concerns of death, and only then was the samurai able to evince the full range of his warrior skills, and to make his mark on the outcome of the battle. Furthermore, should he die in the battle, his name would avoid the terrible black mark of cowardice, with all the reputational, ancestral and spiritual consequences that came with it.

It was acknowledged in samurai thinking, however, that simply to throw away one's life through audacious courage was not a course of action to be recommended automatically. However much a samurai wanted to be recognised for valour – hence the desire to be seen as the first into action on the battlefield – his clan and leaders also needed live fighters, not dead martyrs, if they were ultimately to take the field. So, an acceptance of death did not imply that death should actually be sought as a primary outcome.

RITUAL SUICIDE

Yet there *was* a circumstance in which the samurai would willingly pursue violent death, and that was in the act of *seppuku* or *hara-kiri*, or ritual suicide by slicing open one's abdomen with a blade, cutting from left to right and

▲ *The wife of one of the deceased '47 Ronin' prepares for* jigai *(the female version of* seppuku*); note how her legs are tied together to give dignity in death. (Rama/PD-Art)*

▼ *Ōishi Yoshio publicly commits* seppuku *in 1703, cutting open his belly while his 'second' prepares to behead him. (Shōsen, Hyōgo Prefecture Museum of History/PD-Art)*

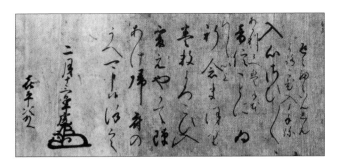

▲ *A letter from Uesugi Kenshin to Uesugi Kagekatsu, in which the writer expresses his regard and concern for the recipient. (AlexHe34/CC-BY-SA-3.0)*

▶ *A samurai prepares himself for the moment of suicide, his* tantō *short sword, poised ready over his belly and his death poem or letter composed in front of him. (PD)*

essentially disembowelling oneself. The means of death were therefore agonising. In recognition of this fact, by the Edo period, the role of the *kaishakunin* ('second') had emerged. The *kaishakunin* – typically a friend or fellow warrior – stood behind the warrior about to commit suicide, and when the knife when into the belly the second would cut off the dying man's head with a swing of his sword. In the *Hagakure*, however, Tsunetomo notes that being a *kaishakunin* was not a favourable position, as performing the job well still meant killing an ally or friend, while botching the effort (a clean decapitation required an excellent blade and much skill) would bring public disgrace. Tsunetomo even recommended that the sword-wielder attempted to leave a connecting length of skin between head and neck, to prevent the head flying off in an undignified spectacle.

The origins of this brutal practice were at first improvisatory rather than ritualistic, and are variously attributed. The bloody honour of being the first to perform *seppuku* might go to the samurai Minamoto no Ta in 1170 following the defeat of his forces at Shirakawa-den, or to the warrior monk Minamoto no Yorimasa at the Battle of Uji in 1180. In these cases, the suicide was a response either to what was perceived as ignominious defeat, or to avoid the indignities of being captured or killed by enemy troops.

Throughout samurai history, many of the recorded instances of *seppuku* were in response to imminent defeat by enemy forces, especially when the strength of the enemy was unequal to anything the samurai could resist. For example, Takeda Katsuyori, once one of the most powerful *daimyō* in Japan and ruler of the Takeda clan, was militarily backed into a corner following a major defeat at the Battle of Nagashino in 1575, after which several allied clans defected to the enemy. Eventually, the combined armies of Oda Nobunaga and Tokugawa Ieyasu gathered against him at Tenmokuzan in 1582, in response to which Katsuyori felt compelled to burn his fortress (Shinpu Castle) and retreat with his family into the mountains. After his attempt to take refuge in the Takeda

stronghold of Iwadono was rebuffed by the Takeda retainer Oyamada Nobushige, Katsuyori's troops kept the pursuing enemy forces off for enough time to allow Katsuyori to commit dignified *seppuku*. We should also note with grim recognition that his wife and son followed Katsuyori in the act of suicide, in the ultimate expression of family martyrdom. It was indeed not uncommon for samurai wives to commit suicide following the death of their husband, or if their husband had died in shame. Unlike the male suicides, the women killed themselves by plunging *tantōō* or *kaiken* blades into their throats, cutting the arteries in the neck and leading to rapid death by exsanguination. If enemy forces were approaching, the woman might also tie her knees together before the act of suicide, so that her body would have some measure of dignity when the troops arrived on the scene. Nor might female suicide be an isolated incident. Following the final defeat of Taira no Tomomori by the Minamoto in 1185, there was a mass suicide of Taira women.

PUBLIC SHAME

A considered but still legitimate reason for *seppuku* was as a response to public shame. Killing oneself in this manner was known as *sokotsu-shi*, which meant 'expiatory suicide'.[20] The shame could come from all manner of sources, least nobly from a sexual exposure or conviction of a humiliating crime, most respectably from poor leadership in battle, leading to ignominious defeat. For example, at the fourth Battle of

COLLECTING HEADS

One of the most gruesome of the samurai warrior practices was the collection of the heads of defeated enemies. The heads were valued as grisly war trophies, and the gathering and eventual presentation of them was framed by a considerable degree of administration and ritual. Once the heads had been taken, either as the cause of death or post-death, military secretaries (*yuhitsu*) would systematically prepare tags to attach to each, giving the identity of the deceased. In the Natori-ryu school's detailed advice on the matter, there were even specifications for the type of handwriting font used to accord with the status of the dead warrior; an upper-class head would, for example, have the honour of block style, while those of the middle class were in cursive font. The head might also be placed into a box, and the name written on the box lid. All the names of the deceased also required entry into the 'Book of the Dead', each line of record listing the date, time of death, name of battle, the location details and some notes on the killing, including who did it and what method was used. The secretaries, who must have been kept nightmarishly busy after a major battle, also had to record the names of dead allied soldiers in the Buddhist death register and also those wounded, in the 'Book of the Injured'. Being able to identify the head was as much a matter of honour as it was of record. During the period of Warring States, it was actually classed as dishonourable for a samurai to take an anonymous head from the battlefield.

Once the heads had been fully recorded, they were prepared for display, being cleaned of blood as best possible, the hair neatened and teeth blackened (blackening teeth was a respected cosmetic process in Japan). Note that the work of tagging and cleaning the heads was often done by women. One such individual remembered that she would actually go to sleep in the presence of all the heads, such was her familiarity with the terrible scene.

Once the heads had been fully prepared, they would usually be displayed in a ceremony for the *daimyō*, so that he could witness the physical scale of his victory. The ceremony could actually take place some considerable time after the killing. For example, in 1574 Oda Nobunaga viewed the heads of his enemies Asakura Yoshikage, Asai Hisamasa and Asai Nagamasa a full year after they had been cut off, a coating of lacquer and gold dust going some way to preserving their appearance.

▲ *A samurai looks fully intent on taking the head of his opponent in battle, although in reality most head removals were post-mortem. (J Marshall, Tribaleye Images/Alamy)*

▼ *The full set of ō-yoroi armour would go a long way to ensuring that a samurai kept his head; note the head, neck and shoulder protection. (Ian Armstrong/CC-BY-SA-2.0)*

Kawanakajima in 1561, the Takeda strategist Yamamoto Kansuke raced alone into the ranks of the enemy army, there facing certain death, when it became apparent that his original plan for victory had failed. Other reasons for suicide included making a political protest, and also killing oneself simply because one's master had been killed or had taken his own life. This latter decision was known as *junshi*, and it was regarded with mixed feelings among philosophers and the ruling classes. Some saw it as the ultimate act of loyalty, others as a pointless waste of one's self. Usually, this was a matter of an individual loyal retainer, or small number thereof, killing themselves in a moment of high emotion. However, these acts could be more considered and on a larger scale, the '47 Ronin' standing out as a salient case (see page 66), and one in which *seppuku* takes centre stage.

PUNISHMENT AND PEACE TREATIES

Of course, *seppuku* might also be imposed on someone involuntarily, as capital punishment for a crime or as part of a dark bargaining strategy between rulers. For example, a

▶ *The 'divine wind' – in reality a supremely timed typhoon – destroys the Mongol fleet during the invasion of Japan in 1281. (Kikuchi Yoosai/Tokyo National Museum/CC-PD-Mark)*

▼ *In an old story, one Jirohei defended an ancient cherry tree to the death, and consequently the tree was imbued with vengeful spirits. (Chronicle/Alamy)*

◀ *The young Toyotomi Hideyoshi leads a small group assaulting the castle on Inaba Mountain, his path framed by elegant moonlight. (National Diet Library/PD-Art)*

THE 47 RONIN

◄ *The graves of the legendary '47 Rōnin' at Sengaku-ji temple, Tokyo. An annual festival is held at the grave site. (Stéfan Le Dû/CC-BY-SA-2.5)*

The story of the 47 Ronin has been told and retold throughout Japanese history, and while embellishments have accrued over time, the core of the narrative is certainly grounded in fact. The story begins in 1701 when Asano Takumi-no-Kami Naganori, the *daimyō* of the Ako Domain in western Honshu, was ordered to prepare a reception for envoys of the emperor, the reception to be held in the court of the shogun (Tokugawa Tsunayoshi) at Edo. To smooth the way, the shogun sent one Kira Kozuke-no-Suke Yoshinaka, a powerful official, to give instruction concerning the etiquette of the event. Yet Naganori fell out with Yoshinaka, the latter feeling that the former did not exhibit enough respect, i.e. Yoshinaka had not greeted the official with the expected 'gifts' (bribes). Naganori did his best to smooth over the incident, but eventually the two men came to blows, Naganori wounding Yoshinaka in the face during a violent tussle. Naganori had made a grievous error in a moment of anger: not only had he attacked one of the shogun's officials, but he had also done so in the grounds of Edo Castle, where it was forbidden even to draw a blade in anger let alone wield one. As punishment, Naganori was ordered to commit *seppuku*, a command with which he complied. Extending the effects of his crime, all Naganori's 300 samurai were made leaderless *ronin*, and Naganori's family lost all their lands and were effectively made destitute.

It was now that a small faction of the *ronin*, 47 in number, began to plot their revenge. Led by the former chief retainer Ōishi Yoshio Kuranosuke, the men dedicated themselves to avenging Naganori by killing Yoshinaka, a plan they knew would ultimately lead to their own deaths at the hands of a vengeful shogunate.

The final act of violence had a long gestation. All 47 men crafted the external appearance of those no longer in samurai service, taking up trades or becoming monks.

Kuranosuke himself acted like a dissolute waster, moving to Kyoto and spending his time in drinking dens and brothels. Yet all the time the *ronin* were gathering intelligence, observing Yoshinaka's movements and finding out, through their trades, about the layout of his house.

Finally, after two years of reconnaissance, during which time Yoshinaka became convinced that he was under no threat, the 47 *ronin* gathered together, armed themselves, and struck. They invaded Yoshinaka's mansion in the early morning hours of a bleak winter day in January, first climbing on the roof and announcing to neighbours what they had come to do. Although Kuranosuke's plan had originally stated that no one was to be harmed except Yoshinaka, the alarm was raised and Yoshinaka's men fought the *ronin* tenaciously; 16 of them were eventually killed in the melee, and 22 wounded. Eventually, the *ronin* subdued the resistance and discovered Yoshinaka. Mindful of the dignity of the prisoner's office, Kuranosuke gave Yoshinaka the option of committing *seppuku*, with Kuranosuke actually acting as the *kaishakunin*. Despite this offer, Yoshinaka did nothing except tremble with fear, so the *ronin* pinned him down and cut off his head with a dagger. They then took the head and placed it on their master's grave in Sengaku-ji temple.

The procedural fallout from Yoshinaka's killing was complicated. By killing Yoshinaka, the *ronin* had acted with the clear precedent of avenging one's master, but only if the vendetta had been registered, which clearly it couldn't be. Furthermore, they had killed a court official, although one with limited popularity; many of the local population were in restrained celebration over what the *ronin* had done. To find a way out of the impasse, the shogunate gave the *ronin* the option of committing *seppuku* instead of being arrested, tried and convicted as criminals. All the *ronin* took this option, and passed into historical legend with their deaths.

▶ *Minamoto no Yoshitsune and others defend themselves at sea during a storm created by the ghosts of dead Taira warriors. (Rijksmuseum/ CC-PD-Mark)*

daimyō, or one of his closest retainers, might be ordered to kill himself to satisfy the requirements of a peace treaty or the cessation of hostilities. In 1590, following the defeat of the Hōjō at Odawara, the victorious Toyotomi Hideyoshi demanded the suicide of the retired *daimyō* Hōjō Ujimasa, plus the exile of his son Ujinao, wiping out the ancestral lineage of the rival clan. As an aside, before his suicide, Ujimasa wrote what were known as 'Death Poems', often a ritualistic and

reflective precursor to the act of *seppuku*. Those written by Ujimasa are particularly haunting and beautiful:

> Autumn wind of eve
> Blow away the clouds that mass
> O'er the moon's pure light.
> And the mists that cloud our mind
> Do thou sweep away as well.
>
> Now I'm about to disappear,
> Wondering how I should grasp it.
> From the emptiness I came,
> Hence I will return there.

The samurai views of life and death are quite alien to much modern social thinking, which places a supreme value on individual human life, not least one's own. Yet the samurai warrior spirit, and its acceptance of death, resurrected itself most unpalatably in the nationalistic Japanese military of the 1920s–40s. During this period, which culminated with Japan's emphatic wartime defeat by the Allies in 1945, *bushido* merged with an appalling cruelty and disdain for others, manifesting itself in such phenomena as the 'Rape of Nanjing' in 1937–38, the appalling treatment of Allied POWs in World War II, and the enthusiastic embrace of suicide tactics both on land and in the air (kamikaze). Despite this, while we can never look back to the samurai and claim that they were beyond barbarity, notions of dignity and civility were still present and respected.

◀ *Samurai photographic portraits in the 19th century are a poignant reflection on an age that had already passed. (CC-PD)*

▼ *Sakanoue no Tamuramaro, a general and shogun of the early Heian period. Japanese art bears much responsibility for shaping the perception of the samurai. (CC-PD-Mark)*

CHAPTER FOUR

SAMURAI ARMOUR AND EQUIPMENT

Samurai armour is usually instantly recognisable, even to those without an interest in the subject. Its combination of lamellar armour, often highly decorative, plus ornate helmets and occasionally garish face masks stands in colourful contrast to the shining and largely plain plate armour that came to dominate warfare in much of medieval Europe. But samurai armour is a complex topic, the apparent recognisability belying a long catalogue of changes, both subtle and profound, over the period of our study.
Our periodisation will follow the broad sweep of the Classical period up to 1467, the era of inter-state conflict from 1467 to 1603 that was the Sengoku *jidai*, and the Edo period, a time of relative peace but continuing martial development.

◄ *A modern re-enactor dresses in full samurai armour. Note the intense volume of lacing, which would become onerously heavy when wet. (Photo Japan/Alamy)*

CLASSICAL-ERA ARMOUR

Japanese armour was certainly complex in both construction and composition, but it was practical. If the armour was well made, it was robust and could withstand the thumps, slashes and stabs of sword, spear, arrow and halberd. A Japanese warrior could legitimately go into battle feeling a sense of physical protection from the armour that encased his body.

LAMELLAR CONSTRUCTION

Although Japanese armour went through some significant shifts in design, for much of its history it was defined by a specific lamellar construction technique. In contrast to plate armour and mail armour, the lamellar armour consisted of numerous small squares of iron or rawhide, typically around 5 × 3cm (2 × 1¼in) in dimensions, tied to each other by

▼ *A dō covered in a thin layer of leather, its decorative finish representing the lamellar scales and lacing of traditional armour. (Samuraiantiqueworld/CC-BY-SA-3.0)*

strips of leather, deerskin or coloured silk thread through holes bored around the periphery, effectively creating tight hinges between each plate. The plates, or lames, were grouped in an overlapping arrangement, to prevent gaps in the armour, and had a high degree of impact resistance. This was enhanced by intelligently mixing the ratios of iron lames to rawhide ones, the iron protecting against cutting or piercing blows, while the rawhide lames, tough in themselves, gave a compression effect, spreading and partially absorbing blunt impacts. Lamellar armour also had a production advantage for countries with limited iron-

▶ *A view of the inside of a* hon iyozane maru dō, *showing the sections of iron scales overlapping one another in an articulated fashion. (Samuraiantiqueworld/CC-BY-SA-3.0)*

producing facilities; the armour type had actually originated in Chinese and Central Asian nomadic tribes, who for reasons of their itinerant existence could not carry with them the fixed large-scale furnaces used for major armour output.

Ō-YOROI ARMOURS

The lamellar scales were built up into larger sections of body armour by arranging them into horizontal rows bound to one another, a solid metal plate at the top of each section. Through these means, the Japanese armour makers were able to produce the *ō-yoroi* (great armours), a full-body protective system that has become one of the defining

▼ *This highly ornate set of 14th-century* ō-yoroi *armour is extensively finished with gilded copper. (Gift of Bashford Dean, 1914/Metropolitan Museum of Art/CC)*

LACQUERING

The lacquering that was such a central application to Japanese armour should not be confused with mere decorative process. The lacquer, known as *urushi*, imparted a deep lustre when applied to leather, wood and metal. Its base material was the sap from the tree *Toxicodendron vernicifluum*, or Chinese lacquer tree, tapped out by cutting horizontal slashes into the bark of a tree more than ten years old, resulting in the thick grey-yellow sap oozing out for collection. This sap was then filtered, heat treated and painted on to the armour artefact, being allowed to dry for up to 24 hours, ideally in warm and humid conditions. Multiple layers of the lacquer would be applied and mixed with other materials such as clay, powdered stone, rice flour, sawdust, chopped straw, mother-of-pearl and colourants, to produce the desired aesthetic and material result. Once fully hardened, the lacquer shell offered extraordinary properties. It was completely waterproof, and thus prevented leather or wood rotting and metal rusting, even in the dampest conditions. It was flexible, hence did not crack under the movements of the armour on the wearer, plus it was extremely tough, resistant to all manner of abrasion and impact. It had a further property of being resistant to most acids and alkalines, thus the sweat of the wearer would not penetrate through to the inner material. The one major downside of the sap was that it was toxic in its liquid state; it contains a compound called urushiol, the same type of irritant oil found in poison ivy. The colour of the lacquer could be adjusted to a degree by adding pigments to the sap when it was still in its liquid state. Carbon or iron compounds would give a black colouration, while iron oxide or vermillion produced red. At the end of the lacquer applications, the surface would usually be polished to a high shine. Other applications of the lacquer included on writing instruments, fans, spear handles, tableware and jewellery.

▲ *An antique samurai* kabuto *(helmet), the plate ridges and large rivets typical of helmet designs up to the late 15th century. (Thierry Bernard/CC-BY-SA-3.0)*

▼ *This Japanese armour diagram by 19th-century weapons historian Wendelin Boeheim shows all the main parts. (Wendelin Boeheim/CC-BY-SA-3.0)*

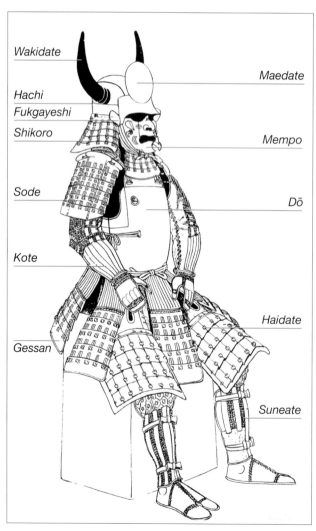

▲ *A view of a samurai helmet showing the* ase nagashi no ana *(drain hole), which allowed collected perspiration to flow away. (Samuraiantiqueworld/CC-BY-SA-3.0)*

images of the samurai. To orientate ourselves around this important armour, and to give ourselves a framework for understanding subsequent changes, we will work through the various elements of the *ō-yoroi* from head to feet, noting along the way some of the critical design considerations that went into this armour. It is important to remember, however, that the subject of Japanese armour is one of academic complexity and subtlety, so space considerations here compel us to rationalise and simplify to some extent.

KABUTO

The helmets, or *kabuto,* worn with the *ō-yoroi* armour are strikingly ornate, although some of what looks like mere decoration to modern eyes did serve a practical function in the context of war fighting. The bowl of the helmet (*hachi*) was constructed of multiple convex plates converging from the helmet rim to a hole at the top called the *tehen*, this being defined and finished by a copper or gilt ring. Various explanations circulate around the *tehen*, including that it was a port for ventilation or even, at a more heavenly level, an aperture through which the spirit of the war god Hachiman could enter, inspiring the samurai to greater feats of martial glory. In reality, the purpose was more likely that it made manufacture simpler. By including the *tehen*, it was far easier to make all plates converge accurately around the crown of the head. For samurai who had long hair, often tied back in a ponytail during combat, the *tehen* was also a useful hole for the flowing hair, and if the samurai wore a long cloth inner cap, excess material could also be gathered through the hole. (Later helmet bowls featured an integral cloth liner.)

Typically, a *hachi* was produced from between eight and 12 metal plates, although certain high-end varieties might climb as high as 20 plates, or even exceed that. There are records of some helmets featuring 120 plates, although such items were more likely used to display wealth and aesthetic sensibility rather than for combat. The curvature of the *hachi*, plus the prominent rivets by which each plate was secured to the next, gave the upper part of the helmet rigidity and strength.

SHIKORO AND MABISASHI

To the rear rim of the helmet was added a neck protector, known as the *shikoro*, a long and flaring section that covered the nape of the neck. The *shikoro* was also of a lamellar construction, with five rows of scales; the top plates at the front of the *shikoro* were turned back and out to form the *fukigaeshi*, projections that prevented downward cuts from enemy blades slicing through the lacing at the helmet. The design of the *shikoro* changed somewhat over time. At first they were relatively narrow and hung nearly vertically from the rim, but over time they became wider and angled more upwards, forming a wide protective pelmet extending out from the back of the samurai's neck.

At the front of the helmet was the leather-covered metal *mabisashi*, a rim extending out to protect the forehead and the brow. Some of the more ornate examples of helmets, typically those worn by senior commanders, featured gilt horns attached to the front of the rim, extending dramatically upwards. Known as *kuwagata*, these did not have the strength to perform any practical armour function, but purely served as an identification of rank and status.

DŌ

The heart of the Japanese armour was the breastplate, or *dō*, the largest and heaviest piece of armour, which wrapped around the wearer's torso. The basic *dō* was formed from five specific sections. Protecting the right side of the torso (the side most exposed by the right-handed use of weapons) was the *waidate*, which was a solid iron plate strapped on to the samurai's body before the rest of the *dō* was fitted. The main structure of the *dō* consisted of four large hinged lamellar sections (these sections were known as the *kusazuri*), which encased the torso and tied at the side, often worn with additional plates to the front and the back. To ensure that the samurai could use his bow properly, without the bowstring snagging on the lamellar plates, a smooth leather panel called a *tsurubashiri* was fitted to the front of the torso section. The whole piece of apparatus was suspended by padded leather shoulder straps.

Extending out from the main body piece of the *dō* were several additional features that gave the cuirass its distinctive

LACING

The colourful lacing by which Japanese armour was tied together was one of its signature features, transforming the plain lacquered metal or rawhide sections into items of striking visual impact. Speaking broadly, there were two styles of lacing. The first, characteristic of expensive sets of *ō-yoroi* armour, was known as *kebiki odoshi* (close-spaced lacing), in which the lamellar plates were almost entirely covered in the rawhide or silk laces, the sections featuring 13 or 14 holes in the plates to facilitate the tight attachment of one plate to those around it. The methods of *kebiki odoshi* not only ensured that the armour presented a visually pleasing appearance, but it also prevented the lames from slipping over one another when the samurai was in action and opening up gaps.

The big problem with *kebiki odoshi* lay in the large volume of fibres used in the construction. When the laces became wet on campaign, they added significantly to the overall weight of the armour, and further restricted the free movement of the armour sections. They also attracted dirt, dried blood, sweat and lice infestations, leading to a variety of skin conditions for the wearer. For this reason, over time the alternative *sugake odoshi* (spaced lacing) became more common. Here, the lacing was visibly more widely spaced, often set in pairs between wider lames. There is much variation in lacing patterns, however. For example, some *dō* showed mixed combinations of both *kebiki odoshi* and *sugake odoshi*, and patterns of horizontal, vertical and diagonal stitching gave the armour maker the ability to express something of his own personality.

▼ *A close-up picture of a* dō *illustrating how small leather scales were laced together in tight-fitting sections. (Samuraiantiqueworld/CC-BY-SA-3.0)*

▲ *A full set of samurai chest armour opened out. In total, this piece consists of more than 500 individual lacquered leather scales. (Samuraiantiqueworld/CC-BY-SA-3.0)*

look. Around the lower edge of the armour were the lower parts of the four *kusazuri*, suspended lamellar sections guarding the torso and upper thighs. At shoulder level were the *sode*, or shoulder guards, hanging flat and square down from the top of the shoulders nearly to the elbow, and

fastened to the back of the armour by an ornamental bow called an *agemaki*. The *sode* were an important feature because the mounted samurai was unable to carry a shield.

DŌ-MARU

The ornate *dō* of *ō-yoroi* armour was not the only torso protection available during this age. The alternatives were largely confined to lower-class samurai or common foot soldiers, but as we shall see, they became increasingly important for the future direction of samurai armour in general. Mounted samurai needed only limited flexibility in their armour, as they fought from a seated position atop their horses. The mounted position also meant that the horse, in a sense, took some of the burden of carrying around 30kg (66lb) of a full set of *ō-yoroi* armour. Dismounted soldiers, by contrast,

◀ Sode *shoulder guards from a 17th-century armour set. (Gift of Bashford Dean, 1914 / Metropolitan Museum of Art/CC)*

required their armour to have a higher degree of flexibility, especially around the upper legs and also around the arms, as they engaged in close-quarters combat. The answer to these requirements was the *dō-maru* (lit. 'torso round'). Like the *ō-yoroi dō*, this wrapped around the body and tied at the right side, but it was closer fitting and was formed in one piece. The *tsurubashiri* was omitted, further lightening the load, and the *kasazuri* were more slender but more numerous – up to seven panels.

The *dō-maru* tended to be worn by samurai retainers with little else in terms of armour protection; indeed, many retainers would follow their masters into battle with no armour at all. Yet the *dō-maru* was a popular and efficient piece of kit, one that the samurai themselves began to adopt. In the second half of the 14th century, furthermore, another type of *dō* emerged: the *haramaki-dō* ('belly-wrap torso').

HARAMAKI-DŌ

To give the sword-, poleaxe- or spear-wielding soldier a greater range of movement in his right arm, the *haramaki-dō* was fastened up the back rather than on the right-hand side of the body. A narrow gap between the meeting point of the armour sections was covered by a separate backplate, known as the *sei ita*. (Because a samurai was never meant to show the enemy his back, this was sometimes referred to as the 'coward's plate'.) Both the *haramaki-dō* and the *dō-maru* were more practical armours as Japanese warfare shifted steadily from the emphasis on cavalry to the foot soldier. As we shall see below, therefore, the samurai themselves came to adopt both these styles of armour, which in turn evolved into what we call *tosei-gusoku* (modern armour).

KOTE

The arms of the enemy were a key target for samurai during battle, as they could be quickly damaged by a short, fast

▼ *A distinctive black* dō-maru haramaki dō, *made from individual scales and opening up at the back. (Samuraiantiqueworld/CC-BY-SA-3.0)*

▲ *An ornate set of samurai armour from the late 18th century illustrates the colourfulness of some armours, courtesy of the lacing, and also hints at the heavy cost of production. (Gift of Bashford Dean, 1914/Metropolitan Museum of Art/CC)*

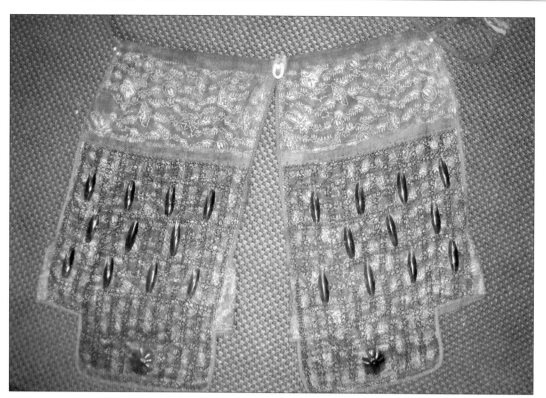

◀ *A* haidate, *or thigh protection, with iron plates and chain armour sewn onto decorative cloth, from the Edo period. (Samuraiantique-world/CC-BY-SA-3.0)*

dō-maru blow following the parry of a spear or sword. Even a relatively minor injury to the arm could render a samurai incapable of wielding his weapons, either taking him out of the fight or setting him up for a lethal blow. The armour protection available for the arms was initially of low sophistication. Early *kote* were little more than fabric sleeves to which were attached armoured plates covering the upper arms, lower arms and the back of the hands, the *kote* tied directly on to the arms themselves. These were as awkward as they sound, and were subsequently given a design upgrade. Most significant, the plates were connected with sections of mail (*kusari*) and also shoulder straps that linked them to the top of the *dō*, thereby alleviating much of the weight of the sleeves from the arms themselves.

SUNEATE

The *suneate* (shin guards) were the last, but essential, piece in the samurai's armour jigsaw. By virtue of the bent-leg posture a samurai would be forced to adopt when in the saddle, the forward-facing shins were especially vulnerable to attack. The *suneate* were constructed from vertical plates connected with mail or rawhide hinges. Some of the earlier examples included large knee extensions, although these were later omitted because they restricted movement in dismounted combat.

▶ *The samurai Yukimori (1543–76), known for his great strength and loyalty, served the Amako warlord during the Sengoku period. Here he is depicted in the* tosei-gusoku *(modern armour). (The Picture Art Collection/Alamy)*

AUXILIARY ARMOURS

◀ *An Edo period iron face mask, to protect the lower face, with an attached chain throat guard. (Samuraiantique-world/CC-BY-SA-3.0)*

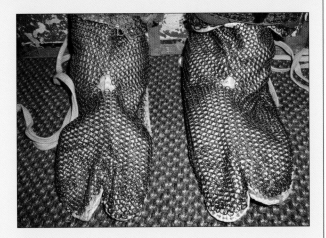

▲ *Armoured 'socks', made from chain armour sewn onto cloth. (Samuraiantiqueworld/CC-BY-SA-3.0)*

Aside from the core pieces of armour, the samurai warrior had a range of minor auxiliary pieces that either supplemented or accompanied the armour set-up.

Nodowa/guruwa – These consisted of a lamellar armour section designed to be tied around the back of the neck, to protect the vulnerable throat area. The difference between the two was that the *guruwa* wrapped fully around the back of the neck, whereas the *nodowa* just shielded the throat area.

Wakibiki – *Wakibiki* were small armoured panels, made from attaching mail, iron or rawhide plates to a cloth backing. They could be placed in various locations, including the armpits or on the front of the *dō*.

Tate-eri – This piece was an armoured standing collar, padded cloth providing cushioning from the weight of the *dō* straps while the fitted armour plates projected against blows to the neck area.

Manju no wa – The *manju no wa* was a form of close-fitting upper-body jacket, lined with mail, or armour plates. When worn, the *manju no wa* protected the shoulders, collarbone and armpits.

Manchira – Similar to the *manju no wa*, the *manchira* was an armour-lined cloth vest, albeit a larger piece that extended over the chest, flanks and back. In some cases, the *manchira* might be worn under civilian clothing for non-combat protection, while larger examples might actually be worn over the *dō* for an additional layer of armour.

Kogake – The *kogake* were armoured socks made of mail or small iron plates, tied on like a sandal with straps over the top of the foot.

◀ A guruwa *throat and neck protector. "Samuraiantiqueworld/CC-BY-SA-3.0)*

▼ *A kikko* manchira *armoured vest. (Samuraiantiqueworld/CC-BY-SA-3.0)*

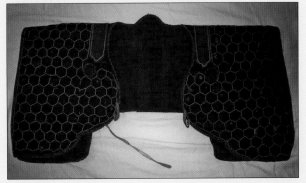

ARMOUR EVOLUTION, 15TH–17TH CENTURIES

As noted in Chapter 1, from the 14th and 15th centuries, Japanese warfare underwent a profound shift in its tactical weight, the bias of action moving towards dismounted combat by large-scale armies dominated in numbers and focus by *ashigaru* foot soldiers.

▲ *A koshiate (sword hanger) used to suspend the sword with the blade facing down,* tachi *style. (Samuraiantiqueworld/ CC-BY-SA-3.0)*

The samurai increasingly fought dismounted, and so it was logical that their requirements for armour changed priorities, producing some significant changes in structural design and overall layout.

By the end of the 14th century, the samurai had largely been persuaded of the value of simpler *dō-maru* and *haramaki* designs. The only samurai who still donned the *ō-yoroi* were those who cleaved to extreme traditionalism, or those who needed something ostentatious for a ceremonial event. Given Japan's very feudal need for a clear distinction between the samurai and the lower ranks, in the 15th and 16th centuries it came to be that the *dō-maru* and *haramaki* were actually the defining armour of the elite. In fact, this distinction was also partly a matter of cost; as armies expanded, the *ashigaru* struggled to meet the costs of acquiring what were still highly expensive bits of kit.

TOSEI-GUSOKU

The beginning of the 16th century saw the next step forward in armour evolution. To avoid the problems intrinsic to the *kebiki odoshi*, and to make an armour that was both more resilient to musket balls and more flexible for soldiers fighting on foot, armourers began to make armour in large sections of solid individual plates, strung together with a significantly reduced amount of lacing in the *sugake odoshi* style. (Often, however, the armourer contrived the appearance of *kebiki odoshi* through the clever use of the lines cut into the surface of the armour plate and patterns of lacquer.) The degree of overlap between the plates was reduced, giving a higher degree of flexibility. The solid iron breastplate of the new *dō* was especially good at deflecting musket balls, although as we shall see in Chapter 5, it was no guarantee against mortal penetration. The whole structure was wrapped in leather and lacquered, making for a smooth, waterproof finish. Furthermore, the depth of the *dō* increased, so that the lower rim of the piece sat more directly on the thighs, reducing some of the weight from the shoulders and thereby providing better mobility to the weapon-wielding arms, as well as enhanced protection for the lower abdomen.

This new style of armour, called *mogami-dō* (after the region where the new armour style was initially developed) or *tosei-gusoku* ('modern armour'), was initially intended for the humbler foot soldiers, but the practicality of its style and the

◄ *Antique ō-yoroi armour. The total weight of a full set of such armour could be upwards of 30kg (66lb). (AlkaliSoaps/ CC-BY-2.0*

▶ *A side view of* hon iyozane maru dō *or chest armour, with no hinge on the right side of the body.* (Samuraiantiqueworld/CC-BY-SA-3.0)

reduced cost also made it appealing to the samurai, who again came to adopt the foot soldiers' armour. Other elements acted as visual signatures. The *sode*, for example, became smaller, flatter and better fitted.

Having embarked on innovation, the armourers kept the momentum. During the mid-16th century, the *okegawa-dō* ('tub-sided cuirass') began to make an appearance. The step forward with this cuirass was that the large plate sections were connected by metal rivets, not lacing, meaning that even the joints between plates had armour-resistant properties. There was an additional advantage of riveting in that the rivets could be pulled out, separating the individual plates to make the armour more convenient for packing. The number of plates making up the *dō* was also significantly reduced by some armourers, in some cases making a cuirass of just two parts, hinged together on the left-hand side, known as the *ni-mai-dō*.

Numbers of *kusazuri* also waxed and waned, the armourers attempting to find the optimum number for maximum leg movement while limiting the gaps between the tassets, which were natural targets for enemy spearmen. The profile of the individual tassets also changed a little, flaring out towards the bottom. Another evolution of this feature was, by the end of the 16th century, to attach the tassets to a separate belt, rather than to the *dō* itself, this belt being removable when the armour required packing away.

The new expanses of smooth armour plate offered plenty of opportunities for armourers to display their creative sensibilities, either through imitations of traditional lamellar armour and *kebiki* lacing, or through some rather more peculiar modifications of the armour plate. One example was the *hotoke-dō*, in which the plate over the front torso was

▼ *The* haidate, *a split-panel apron, provided flexible protection for the thighs and groin, two areas vulnerable to sword or spear strikes.* (Samuraiantiqueworld/CC-BY-SA-3.0)

bulged outwards and then covered and lacquered smooth, to create the appearance of the cuirass being the bulging, curved belly of a Buddhist monk. Some armour designers took the verisimilitude further and also included a pair of saggy male breasts, not an image with the most martial connotations for a modern audience, but at the time evoking a mix of warrior practicality and spiritual devotion. But there was also simplicity as well: the *sendai-dō* was on a plain cuirass of vertical plates, and was worn by the army of the samurai warrior and leader Date Masamune.[21]

HELMETS AND FACE MASKS

The modernisation of armour from the 16th century extended to samurai helmets. *Kabuto* wandered freely across the spectrum of design practicality, from simply mass-production headgear, plain in style and design, to high-value examples of the most outlandish decoration. Leaning towards the lower end of that spectrum, a significant developed in c. 1550 was the production of the first *zunari kabuto*, or 'head-shaped helmet'. As we have seen, *kabuto* varied significantly in the number of plates it took to craft the dome – there are some examples of 120 plates of more (although these were unlikely to be taken into the battlefield, being more for display). The line where an individual plate met with the one by its side could be styled in a number of ways. A *hari bachi kabuto*, for example, had smooth transitions between each plate, whereas the *suji bachi kabuto* had the metal flared out in definite ridges.

Zunari kabuto

The *zunari kabuto* was produced by just three plates without a *tehen*; instead of the hole, a longitudinal ridge ran over the full length of the helmet bowl. The relation of this ridge to the helmet's peak (either overlapping the top of the peak or the peak overlapping it), as well as the flared contours of the peak itself, distinguished some local styles. The *zunari kabuto* was primarily a budget helmet aimed at arming the mass of soldiery. Its emergence was made possible by new developments in metalworking, which enabled the armourer better to manipulate large sheets of iron.[22]

Two styles of neck guard were attached to the *zunari kabuto*: 1) *etchu zunari shikoro*, with a horizontal lower edge, and 2) the *hineno shikoro* that extended further down to provide deeper protection to the back of the neck and the shoulders. (One noticeable general point about the *shikoro* of the *tosei-gusoku* was that the *shikoro* were now angled down flatter to the sides and back of the neck, rather than flaring out towards the horizontal, as with some earlier styles.) Yet for all its simplicity, it was a robust and practical battlefield

▲ *The most arresting element of this suit of armour is the prominent* kabuto maedate *crest on the helmet, given as stylised deer horns. (PRAWNS/Alamy)*

▲ *A magnificent set of ō-yoroi armour. Note the* fukigaeshi *armour sections extending out either side of the face, from the rim of the helmet. (Ian Armstrong/CC-BY-SA-2.0)*

▶ *The lacing of samurai armour was not only a design element, but it also identified the warrior's clan affiliation. (World History Archive/ Alamy)*

helmet, so much so that, once again, it gravitated on to the heads of safety-minded samurai and *daimyō* for combat use, despite the lower-class connotations that came with it. To give the helmets a more authoritative appearance, the samurai would often transform them with heavy and colourful decoration, such as wood-carved faces or papier-mâché animals. Although these figures would have added nothing practical in terms of head protection, they would certainly have helped the samurai or commander to stand out from the common herd. Entire helmets might also be coloured in vivid shades of lacquer, such as deep crimsons or solid blacks.

Eboshi kabuto

Another striking style of helmet for the samurai was the *eboshi kabuto*. The *eboshi* part of the phrase referred to a tall cloth cap, its crown slightly folded down, that was a very common form of daily headgear for Japanese men up until about the middle of the 15th century. They began to fall out of

use as the fabric stiffened and made them more uncomfortable, plus the fashion for displaying *sakayaki* (shaving the front of the head) arose. Given their new talents in metalworking, however, some Japanese armourers fashioned metal imitations of the *eboshi* in helmet form. These helmets stood up tall and proud on the head, replicating the lofty cloth crown in metal. A sophisticated adaptation of the style was the *kazaori-eboshi* or 'wind-folded *eboshi*', in which the armourer made a crease in the crown to given the effect of it folding under the strength of the wind. Prominent figures known to wear the *eboshi kabuto* were Maeda Toshiie (c. 1538–1599), a general of Oda Nobunaga, and the *daimyō* Katō Kiyomasa (1562–1611).

Because of the lavish nature of much Japanese armour, particularly when displaying intensive lacing and colourful ornamentation, it might be assumed that the armour did not have the same resilience as the gleaming plate of European medieval and Renaissance pieces. This was far from the

---

FACE MASKS

Given the extensive wrappings provided by Japanese armour, exposed – and therefore vulnerable – parts of the body were few and far between. The face was one of them, thus, for those who could afford them, and who also wished to strike additional fear into the hearts of their enemies, there were some aggressive-looking face-mask options. These were known collectively as *men yoroi* (face armour – also *mengu* or *menpō*), and were often rendered in ferocious expressions (if they included facial features) from sections of rawhide, although higher-ranking samurai commanders leaned towards mask expressions of greater serenity and wisdom. There were varieties that covered the entire face, called *somen*, but they were not widespread or popular, as the majority of samurai

understandably wanted unimpeded breathing and eyesight during battle. The most basic of the masks was the *etchubo*, a piece of formed rawhide that wrapped just around the lower chin. The *hanbo*, meanwhile, covered both the chin and the cheeks, while the *happuri* flipped things around and shielded the cheeks and the forehead. One of the more popular styles of the *men yoroi* was the *menpō*, which shielded the entire lower half of the face, including the nose and mouth. The *menpō* included an attached neck plate (*yodarekake*) that extended down over the front of the throat. A spin on the *menpō* was the *reisei men* ('fierce men') type, in which the mouth of the mask was given angry-looking teeth while the nose was adorned with a flourishing and robust false moustache.

◄ *A particularly striking full-face* men yoroi, *displayed in the Asian Art Museum of San Francisco. (Marshall Astor/CC-BY-SA-2.0)*

case. Although Japanese armour certainly went a long way to broadcasting the status of the wearer, much practical intelligence had gone into the design and, if properly fitted, the armour would have dramatically increased the samurai's chances of surviving an armed encounter. There are accounts in which, after a battle, samurai removed their armour, only to have musket balls drop out, the balls having penetrated the plates but at the cost of so much momentum that they did not pierce the wearer's skin. We also have surviving examples of *dō* and *kabuto* that are dented with tested firings of arrows or muskets; the armourer knew full well that his products had to stand up to the threats. At the same time, the visual exceptionalism of Japanese armour has become a signature of the samurai, as much so as the samurai sword.

▶ *An example of the* happuri *facial armour, designed to protect the forehead and the cheeks. (Samuraiantiqueworld/ CC-BY-SA-3.0)*

▼ *An example of the* hotoke-dō *armour, made from iron plate rather than individual scales, and giving better protection against firearms. (Samuraiantiqueworld/CC-BY-SA-3.0)*

▼ *This* karuta tatami dō *armour provided a lightweight and folding alternative to the bulkier and heavier types. (Samuraiantiqueworld/CC-BY-SA-3.0)*

CHAPTER FIVE

WEAPONS AND FIGHTING SKILLS

History has ascribed the samurai sword with a near mystical significance. Manufactured by master craftsmen, the species of samurai sword – the *katana*, *tachi*, *wakizashi*, *tantō* (the latter more of a dagger) – were forged to the most exacting standards, giving them a deserved reputation as being some of the finest blades in history. To learn how to wield the sword properly in battle, with genuine skill and poise, was a journey of many decades; those samurai who mastered the sword belonged to a martial elite as well as a social one.

◄ *A mounted samurai draws his bow; note the dismounted female warrior by his side, armed with the naginata, a weapon often associated with female use.*
(Lepidlizard / PD-Self)

THE SAMURAI ARSENAL

The samurai had a variety of tools with which to make war, far more than just the sword with which they have become historically associated. The sword was a close-range weapon, but there were other weapons offering a stand-off distance, including the bow and the arquebus, but also the lengthy *naginata* pole arm and *yari* spear.

In the great manual of Japanese swordsmanship, *The Book of Five Rings*, author Miyamoto Musashi made it clear that the samurai warrior had to be conversant with all weapons at his disposal, the bow, gun, spear and halberd. But, he notes:

> Nevertheless, it is logical to speak in martial arts in specific reference to the long sword. Because society and individuals are both ordered by way of the powers of the long sword, therefore the long sword is the origin of martial arts. When you have attained the power of the long sword, you can single-handedly prevail over ten men. When it is possible to overcome ten men single-handedly, then it is possible to overcome a thousand men with a hundred, and to overcome ten thousand men with a thousand.[23]

To accomplish such level of skill, however, required not just endless realistic practice with the sword, but also a deep

appreciation of the spiritual principles of balance, harmony, reaction and awareness that underpinned swordsmanship. To be a true warrior, Musashi clarified, you should, 'Let your inner mind be unclouded and open, placing your intellect on a broad plane.' Wielding the sword was, in essence, about the perfect blend between steel and mind.

In this chapter, we will give full consideration to the tools and tactics of swordsmanship. But as Musashi himself hints, the sword is not the full picture – far from it. If we were to trace a very broad evolution of weapon use in samurai, we would find that in the Classical period (up to 1467), the dominant weapon of the samurai was the bow, typically fired from horseback with impressive dexterity, whether attacking or retreating. Only once the battle had devolved to a close-quarters action on foot did the samurai dismount and reach for his sword. The main arm of the retainers fighting alongside the samurai was the *naginata*, a heavy-bladed type of halberd (described in detail on page 91) or, less commonly, a *kikuchi yari* straight spear.

Matters changed following the Japanese encounter with the Mongols during the 13th century. The Mongols' contrasting form of warfare, which emphasised fighting on foot in unit formations, rather than centring on the individual warrior, resulted in a progressive shift away from horseback archery among the samurai. Although the samurai often still fought mounted, with the more transitional tactics of mounted and dismounted combat, the sword came more to the fore in samurai combat, as did the *yari* (spear), *naginata* and another heavy pole weapon called the *nagamaki*.

Another change came during the Sengoku *jidai*, as the *ashigaru* were recruited in ever-greater numbers, and whose mass presence became the vanguard force in battle. The *ashigaru*, typically farmers or peasants by trade, did not have the martial heritage or the training to wield anything as sophisticated as a samurai sword. (There were also social restrictions on sword ownership anyway; only the samurai were permitted to carry dual swords in their belts.) They were armed principally with the *yari*, a basic bladed weapon designed for a simple thrust attack, and the bow. Then, in the 16th century, came revolution for the *ashigaru*, as the *yari* were progressively (although never completely) replaced by matchlock firearms. As we have noted elsewhere, firearms fundamentally changed the nature of warfare in Japan, and the samurai were not immune to these shifts. Indeed, from

◄ *A collection of samurai arms and armour made between 1500 and 1800. (A. Astes/Alamy)*

MIYAMOTO MUSASHI (c. 1584–1645)

Miyamoto Musashi is a landmark figure in the history of the samurai and Japanese martial arts, although the historical details of his life are somewhat patchy, and it is difficult to distil fact from legend. Looking at his own autobiography, as recounted in *The Book of Five Rings*, he was born in Harima Province, and evidently martial arts and swordsmanship overshadowed his earliest years. At the age of 13 he fought his first duel, with a fighter called Arima Kihei, then went on to defeat an even more respected opponent, one Akiyama of Tajima Province. Evidently warming to his skill with the sword, by his early 20s Musashi had moved to Kyoto, where he engaged in duels with dozens of protagonists from the leading sword schools, defeating them all in turn while honing his craft. It is said that he was particularly skilled in fighting with two swords, one in each hand, and in defeating blade-armed opponents with nothing more than a bamboo training sword.

For all his mastery of the sword, Masashi evokes a genuine humility. Although a victorious fighter in his youth, and in numerous later battles allied to the Toyotomi clan (although his later allegiance, from 1640, was to the Hosokawa clan), he kept pursuing the warrior pilgrimage, searching for the 'deeper principle' of martial arts that, by

his own admission, he only arrived at when aged about 50 years old. It was in 1643 that he began writing the *Gorin no shô* (*The Book of Five Rings*), completing it in the year he died. The deep spirituality of this work, in addition to the obviously intimate understanding of swordsmanship and combative body dynamics, has ensured that his ideas still reach a wide audience to this day.

this time we start to see images of samurai themselves holding matchlocks. Musashi also makes clear that firearms were integrated into the Japanese arsenal at all levels of society. Yet the sword became the samurai's defining tool of martial identity, right through to the 19th century and beyond.

◄ *In this fascinating colourised photo from 1870, modern samurai are all armed with* naginata *and* tantō *short swords. (Felice Beato / CC-PD-Mark)*

► *A collection of antique Japanese matchlock rifles (*tanegashima*), as displayed in Himeji Castle. (pdeaudney/ CC-BY-2.0)*

BOWS AND ARCHERY

The Japanese bow was, like the English longbow, a weapon that took years of consistent practice to master. Although they began back in prehistory as self-bows (made from a single piece of wood), by roughly the 9th century they had developed into composite weapons, with effective ranges well in excess of 100m (109yds).

The Japanese bow was of composite type, utilising the wood from deciduous trees as the core of the bow shaft, backed and fronted by glued strips of bamboo, to improve the compression and elasticity of the draw and release. Unlike the composite bows of Central Asia, which used horn and animal sinew in their laminations, the Japanese *yumi* or *kyo* bows were vulnerable to delamination, as bamboo was not an ideal material for gluing. To reduce the overall stresses on the bow, therefore, they were made particularly long – about 2m (6ft 6in) in length – and were reinforced by spaced rattan bindings. The whole bow was also heavily lacquered, to prevent damp weather from penetrating the wood and weakening the glue. The grip was not located centrally in the bow, but rather in the lower half, to make the weapon more convenient when manoeuvring over a horse's neck.

▼ *An 18th-century woodcut print depicts samurai hunters (bottom) armed with bow and arrows. (Granger Historical Picture Archive/Alamy)*

Bowstrings were made from waxed and woven plant fibre, typically hemp or rami.

ARROWS AND ARROWHEADS

The arrows fired from the bow were made from bamboo, straightened over a charcoal fire and then trimmed and polished. The fletching (*hane*) came courtesy of eagle (especially the sea eagle) or pheasant feathers, three or four fletchers being typical, the higher number tending to be reserved for arrows with larger and heavier heads. The judicious bow maker would ensure that he mixed feathers from both the right and the left wings of the bird, to impart the correct spin stabilisation. The fletchers were glued to the shaft and tied in place with cord; further reinforcing bindings were applied just in front of the nock and just behind the arrow head, these helping to prevent the arrow shaft splitting

▼ *This model of a samurai figure gives a good impression of the sheer length of the bow; the bulk of the length was above the handle joint. (Tom Milani/Alamy)*

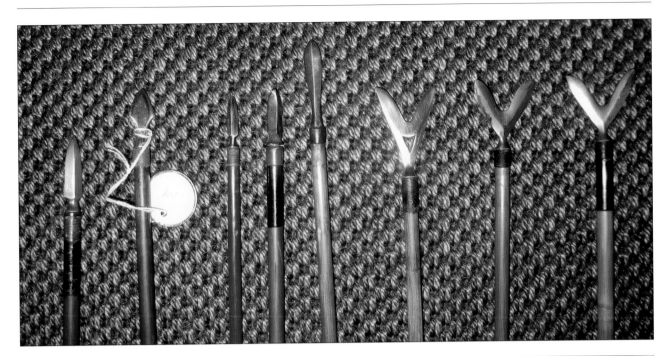

under the tension of the drawn bow or upon impact with the target. The arrowhead was affixed via a tang, inserted into a hole in the tip of the shaft, while the nock (*hazu*) was made from goat or deer horn.

A variety of steel arrowheads (*ya no ye*) were on offer. The most common types had lozenge or square cross-section profiles, these acting like knives and chisels respectively to puncture through enemy body armour. Flat, broad *yanagi-ba* (willow-leaf) arrowheads were also often cut through with surprisingly ornate patterns, the decoration both increasing the prestige of the archery set while also practically lightening the arrowhead for extra flight distance. These ornate and expensive arrows were often specially selected for firing at high-profile enemy targets, such as commanders or distinguished samurai.

Another type of arrowhead was the forked *karimata*, the dual point intended to increase the likelihood of a strike on a vital part of the body. Sometimes these arrows also featured a bulbous *kaburi-ya* device fitted just behind the arrowhead. Made from wood or ivory, the sharp whistle these emitted as they flew through the air was used both as a signalling noise for friendly troops and to intimidate enemy forces.

QUIVERS

The arrows would be carried in a quiver, these ranging from either a simple fabric pocket for the sharp arrowheads, with the arrow shafts supported in a wooden or rope frame, up to beautiful animal skin *utsubo*, which kept the arrows almost completely enclosed and protected them from the weather. Another common accoutrement of the samurai archer was a wicker or wooden reel hung from the belt, this holding a coiled spare bowstring.

ARCHERY SKILLS

Archery, like swordsmanship, required years of aching practice to embed itself with any proficiency. The archer first

▲ *A selection of the various arrowheads, known as* yajiri *or* yanone. *The three heads on the right are the distinctive* karimata. *(Samuraiantique-world/CC-BY-SA-3.0)*

▶ *A beautifully crafted* utsubo *style of* yebira *quiver. It was important to keep arrows as protected as possible from environmental influences. (Samuraiantique-world/CC-BY-SA-3.0)*

▲ *This illustration, showing the night attack on Yoshitsune's residence at Horikawa, shows several of the major classes of samurai weaponry. (Lepidlizard/PD-Self)*

had to embed the muscle memory of simply drawing and releasing the bow with complete control, and judging the rise and drop of an arrow over range to the target. The Japanese technique for drawing the bow was to raise it high (i.e. over the head of the horse) and then lower the bow while pushing

▶ *Samurai practise their archery shooting positions. Note that the three men at the bottom are again wearing hunting gear. (Granger Historical Picture Archive/Alamy)*

▼ *A modern practitioner demonstrates the traditional skills of* kisha, *or mounted archery, which requires exquisite timing and coordination. (Arif Iqball Photography, Japan/Alamy)*

the hands apart until the bowstring was by the archer's right ear. The Japanese archers gripped the bowstring with the thumb, the first fingers of the draw hand, then pressed down on the thumbnail to keep the grip in place. Naturally, this action was somewhat hard on the fingers, so special gloves were used for training, featuring a horn-lined thumb, while in combat the samurai wore deerskin gloves, which also allowed them to control a sword or pole weapon.

The samurai would spend many an hour on horseback practising their archery skills, firing at small wooden targets while they galloped, twisting in the saddle and also judging the rise and fall of the horse, coordinating all the physical actions and mental computations into the perfect moment to release the bowstring. Mastering this confidence was critical if the samurai was to come out alive from archery duels, in which individual samurai rode at each other repeatedly, trying to score the fatal blow. Another training method was the sport of *yabusame*, still practised today, in which the archer gallops down a track 255m (280 yards) long and fires a blunt arrow at a special board, which resonates with sound when struck accurately. There was an alternative archery sport called *inuoumono*, in which a selection of unfortunate dogs was released into a circular enclosure some 15m (50ft) across, and samurai rode around the perimeter shooting the dogs. In a nod to humanity, the arrows later became blunt or padded rather than 'live', giving the dogs nasty bruises rather than fatal injuries.

NAGINATA

The king of the Japanese pole weapons was the *naginata*. It was used by all types of Japanese warrior, from samurai to *ashigaru*, and was especially favoured by the *sohei*. Like the European glaive, the *naginata* consisted of a long shaft, anywhere from 1.2 to 2.4m (4–8ft) in length, to which was affixed a curved, single-edged blade that measured 30–60cm (1–2ft).

The blade was fitted to the shaft via a tang, held in place with a wooden peg called a *meguki*. As the wood just below the blade was subject to the most impact stress – this area was called the *tachiuchi* – it was reinforced with a set of metal bands or rings, which were then in turn wrapped with cord (*san-dan maki*). The shaft had a coating of lacquer, to give better adhesion between the hands and the wood as well as to provide weatherproofing, and many *naginata* also had cord or leather wrapping around the shaft to provide a grip surface. The end of the shaft terminated in a metal end cap known as the *ishizuki*. When the weapon was not in use, the blade was protected by a wooden scabbard.

The *naginata* was not a weapon for the physically weak. The blade alone could weigh the best part of 1kg (2.2lb), and with the weight of the hardwood shaft added it took strength in the chest, shoulders and arms to wield the weapon accurately while keeping it under control. Recognising this fact, the makers of *naginata* had, by the end of the Classical period, implemented measures to reduce weight, such as making the blades shorter and lighter.

The *naginata* was held out in front of the warrior, always with a two-handed grip, although the grip hands could frequently switch positions to adjust to the technique. To deliver a blow, it could be thrust out towards the opponent, either to deflect the enemy's weapon or to deliver a cut to the arms, shoulders, neck or face with the razor-sharp blade. (*Naginata* blades could be manufactured to the same

◄ *An antique Japanese* naginata *and its wooden* saya, *the sheath used to protect the blade when not in use. (Samuraiantiqueworld/CC-BY-SA-3.0)*

▼ *Here we see the metal rings (*naginata dogane *or* semegane) *that reinforce the shaft of the weapon over the tang. (Samuraiantiqueworld/CC-BY-SA-3.0)*

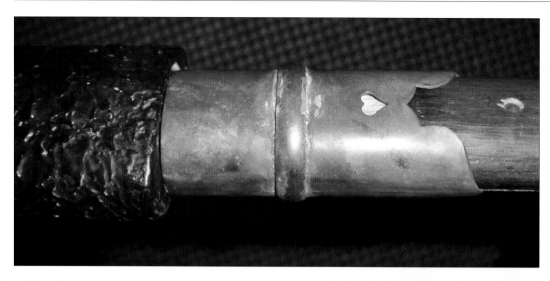

◄ *The* sakawa *metal sleeve was an alternative reinforcing device to the* naginata dogane. Samuariantique-world/CC-BY-SA-3.0)

FEMALE WARRIORS

An often-overlooked element of the samurai were the *onna-bugeisha*, female samurai warriors. Their history dates back to the 2nd and 3rd centuries AD, when noble women learned fighting skills not only to defend hearth and home in violent times, but also on occasions to take their place on the battlefield. Although during the Heian period female warriors were few in number, their number increased significantly during the Kamakura period, and especially during the Sengoku *jidai*. With the

samurai men often away campaigning, and with the likelihood of enemy predation on the towns and villages, women trained earnestly, especially with the *naginata*, to act as their own self-defence force. Their skills became much respected. Furthermore, some women also accompanied their menfolk to war, fighting with a power and skill that brought equal respect. Great named *onna-bugeisha* include Tomoe Gozen, Nakano Takeko and Hōjō Masako. Tomoe Gozen, for example, was the servant of Minamoto no Yoshinaka, but at the Battle of Awazu in 1184 she showed the highest level of fighting skills, at one point killing one of the enemy's strongest warriors. An account of her in the *Heike Monogatari* describes her as:

> …especially beautiful, with white skin, long hair, and charming features. She was also a remarkably strong archer, and as a swords-woman she was a warrior worth a thousand, ready to confront a demon or a god, mounted or on foot. She handled unbroken horses with superb skill; she rode unscathed down perilous descents. Whenever a battle was imminent, Yoshinaka sent her out as his first captain, equipped with strong armor, an oversized sword, and a mighty bow; and she performed more deeds of valor than any of his other warriors.'[24]

The age of the *onna-bugeisha* began to pass in the Edo period, when male samurai moved steadily away from their warrior lifestyles, and, as decorous society took over, women were expected to embody household virtues rather than martial ones.

◄ *Ishi-jo, wife of Oboshi Yoshio, one of the '47 Rōnin', demonstrates her skill with the* naginata. *(Utagawa Kuniyoshi/CeCILL)*

▲ *Samurai warriors practise their spear fighting skills, using* yari *with padded tips to enable them to deliver strikes on their training partners. (Granger Historical Picture Archive/Alamy)*

standards as samurai swords.) The weapon was also swung powerfully in a chopping action, aiming at the legs, flanks, neck and skull, the angle of attack varying from a horizontal sweep to a vertical drop.

The *naginata* was a practical weapon for hand-to-hand fighting, especially as it provided a stand-off distance that the enemy weapon might not have. One of its other useful applications was a weapon to attack or unseat enemy cavalry. A whistling, chopping swing from a *naginata* could easily amputate a limb of either horse or rider; indeed, it was largely because of the presence of *naginata* that samurai armour began to incorporate leg greaves. Conversely, the *naginata* was just as useful for the cavalryman, the length of the weapon meaning that he could comfortably hit warriors at ground level without having to lean excessively.

The declining use of the *naginata* began in the 16th century, as firearms and *yari* began to take over as the primary weapons of the foot soldier. Interestingly, the *naginata* nevertheless persisted as the weapon of choice for samurai women, as part of their home-defence kit. The *naginata* was felt to be particularly suitable for women because its length meant that they could keep physically stronger opponents at distance.

NAGAMAKI

An alternative to the *naginata*, the *nagamaki* belongs more to our discussion of swords starting on page 95, as it was in effect an extra-large sword, albeit with the hilt/tang the same length or longer than the blade. In fact, the *nagamaki* evolved from an earlier type of sword known as the *odachi* or 'great sword', a prodigious and rather impractical weapon, so long it sometimes required an assistant to draw it from its scabbard. The *nagamaki* name itself means 'long wrapping', referring to the cord or leather wrapping around the hilt, although some specimens appear to have had no wrapping at all. The overall length of the weapon varied according to construction, but some could measure up to 2.5m (8ft 2in), and weighed more than 3.5kg (7lb 11oz). The *nagamaki* was principally an anti-cavalry weapon for infantry troops, its design offering a blend of tactical properties somewhere between sword, spear and halberd.

▼ *A* nagamaki *and scabbard. Wielded with two hands, the weapon could inflict massive slicing injuries.* (Samuariantiqueworld/CC-BY-SA-3.0)

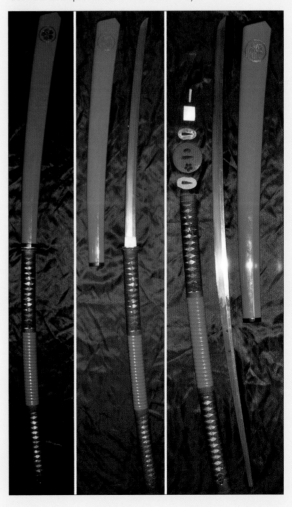

YARI

Among the *ashigaru*, the chief weapon was the *yari*, but it was also popular among the samurai class, including samurai generals. *Yari* offered the practicality of being simple to use as two-handed thrusting weapons, as intimidating to enemy infantry as they were to cavalry.

When presented in massed ranks, the *yari* made for a formidable shock weapon and defensive tool. There was something of an arms race during the Sengoku and Edo periods, when the length of the spears increased as each army sought stand-off advantage, although the lengths to which the later spears aspired challenged their practicality as weapons. So, for example, while the earliest spears would have measured about 3.4m (11ft 2in), by the era of Oda Nobunaga in the late 16th century there were specimens that reached up to 5.6m (18ft 4in) long.

In its simplest form, the *yari* consisted of a straight hardwood (red oak was typical) shaft terminating in a short blade (*hosaki*), the blades usually having parallel sides (although in some rare examples the tip is flared) and a triangular or lozenge-shaped cross-section profile. A metal sleeve known as a *sakawa* protected the wooden section where the blade's tang was inserted into the haft. Like the other weapons mentioned above, the haft was lacquered, and interspersed along its length were metal reinforcing rings, as well as a cord wrapping that provided a grip section. The bottom of the haft was capped with an *ishizuki*, which would sometimes feature a hole for attaching a *tenawa*, or 'rope to keep in the hand'. The rope was particularly useful for spear retention and retraction, particularly when fighting against an enemy on physically lower ground, or where the spear might sink into soft earth, such as might occur when fighting in marshland.

Over time, the *yari* acquired some moderate sophistication through additional features. The *jumonji yari* featured two additional blades projecting out at right angles from the base of the main spear, forming a cross-pattern that increased the cutting area, enabled the user to inflict injuries with sideways movements, and provided a device for hooking the limbs and necks of infantry and cavalry and pulling them off balance. *Yari* might also feature a *hadome*, an iron crossbar located just above the grip wrap, used to stop or trap enemy blades as they slid along the haft.

▲ *The head of a* jumonji yari; *all edges of the three blades would be sharpened, making it a multi-directional weapon. (Rama/CeCILL)*

◄ *Three variants of the* yari, *including one (left) with a crossbar that could be used for trapping the opponent's blade or polearm. (Rama/CeCILL)*

SAMURAI SWORDS

Looking beyond the many cheap reproductions available today, the samurai sword of history represents a moment of near perfection in the evolution of edged weapons. The challenge that the Japanese swordsmiths faced was largely that of all swordmakers: to construct a blade that was the perfect blend of hardness and flexibility.

A sword needed to be forged with the greatest possible hardness, which gave a strong and resilient cutting edge, while at the same time giving the blade enough 'softness' to flex under impacts without breaking. A sword that is too hard throughout will be brittle and will tend to shatter when it is struck by another metal weapon; a sword that is too soft can bend rather than shatter, and its cutting edge will quickly become blunt.

Before explaining the process of sword construction, a brief typology of Japanese swords is required.

TYPES OF SWORD

The blade length of a Japanese sword was measured in *shaku*, a unit of measurement equivalent to 303mm (11.9in). The most well known of the samurai sword types, the *katana*, had a blade length of more than 2 *shaku*. The way in which a samurai sword was carried also had a bearing on its identity. The *katana* was worn with the edge facing upwards when in its scabbard, the scabbard inserted into the sash on the samurai warrior's left hip. The older *tachi*, used during the Heian to the Muromachi periods, was generally slightly longer

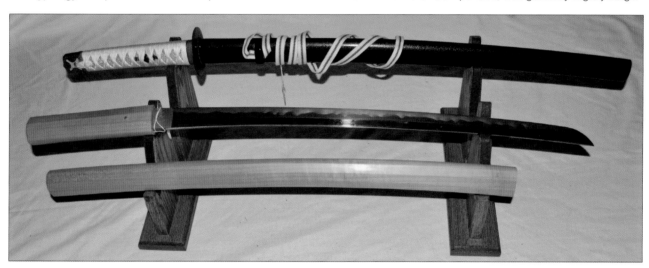

▲ *A 17th-century* katana, *with a* koshirae *mounting at the top and a* shirasaya *at the bottom, the latter just used for sword storage.* (Samuariantiqueworld/CC-BY-SA-3.0)

▼ *A complete samurai* daishō, *featuring* katana *and* wakizashi *swords, made by separate swordsmiths.* (Samuariantiqueworld/CC-BY-SA-3.0)

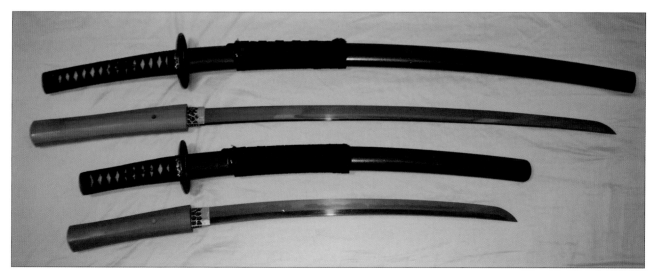

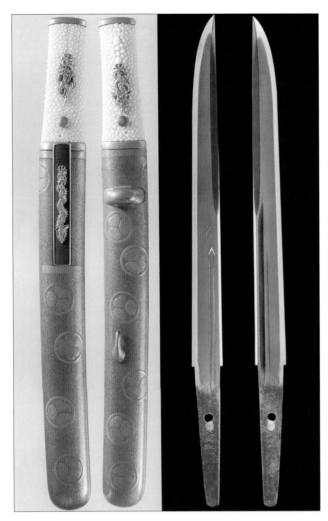

▲ *A tantō with signature (mei) of Shintōgo Kunimitsu, a famous swordmaker who specialised particularly in making tantō. (Sano Art (CC-BY-SA-2.5)*

and more curved than the *katana*, but its name arose more from its style of mount, the scabbard being suspended from rings, with the edge of the blade presented downwards. The evolutionary link between the *tachi* and the *katana* was the *uchigatana*, which ushered in the age of wearing the blade

▼ *A daishō set of Japanese sword storage mounts (shirasaya) for a katana (top) and wakizashi (bottom). (Samuariantiqueworld/CC-BY-SA-3.0)*

presented upwards, although in many ways the actual difference between the *katana* and the *uchigatana* is semantic rather than reflected in major physical variations.

Another particularly important blade is the *wakizashi*, a shorter weapon (blade length was 1–2 *shaku*) that was worn alongside the *katana* in a pairing known as *daishō* (literally 'big–little'). Some samurai would train themselves to fight with both weapons at the same time, one in each hand. The final key samurai blade was the *tantō*, essentially a dagger with a blade length of less than 1 *shaku*.

The reason behind the shift from blade-down to blade-up position is typically that the blade-up configuration was better suited to the days when samurai fought primarily mounted, the angle of the sword being easier to draw in the seated position. However, once samurai combat descended more to ground level, the *tachi* mount became awkward, slapping against the samurai's hip as he moved, a problem overcome by fixing the scabbard semi-rigidly to the hip. Also, by having the blade now facing upwards, a faster draw and double-handed downward cut was possible, which could give a brief window of advantage to the samurai against a slower enemy.

While in civilian dress, the *katana* and the *wakizashi* were worn together in the waist sash, but once armour was donned this arrangement became impractical, so the samurai reverted to belts or sword hangers (*koshiate*) in much the same way as the *tachi* configuration. Furthermore, when wearing armour, the samurai would also pair the *katana* with the more convenient *tantō*, mirroring the practice of warriors during the Classical period.

CONSTRUCTION
The beginning of the journey from a crude block of iron ore (specifically magnetite) to a completed samurai sword began with the smelting process.

Smelting
This was performed over several days using charcoal as fuel, the swordsmith continually managing the influx of ore, charcoal and air to control the resultant carbon content. The output of this process was a slag of iron and steel known as *tamahagane*. At the right moment, the furnace was broken up and the *tamahagane* dragged out, allowed to cool, then flattened and broken up with a hammer to create small, flat plates. The swordsmith would select the best examples of these plates, and separate them into a pile that would be

Hammering and folding

The smith now had the blocks of steel he would use for his sword. To remove impurities and excess carbon he then proceeded to one of the most famous processes of the sword construction, heating the metal, cutting part way through, folding and hammering out the blocks repeatedly – an activity that removed any remaining impurities from the steel, making its structure more consistent. This process required great judgement, born of long experience and skill, the smith directing assistants with hammers to make judicious blows. The result could be a blade that, through mathematical doubling and tripling, could have literally millions of layers within its steel. The process also reduced the volume of the steel by up to 75 per cent, the final steel remaining approaching the actual weight of the sword blade. The smith might also take multiple separate sections of finished steel, weld them together, and then refold to create the hard outer skin of the sword, known as the *kawagane*.

Forming the sword

The process by which the folded steel blocks were forged into a sword varied according to the skill of the smith and the value of the final sword. At the top end of cost and sophistication, for example, were swords formed from four different hardnesses of steel, for applying to the edge, sides, back and core. More typically, however, the smith would weld *uagane* steel around or on to a *shingane* core; for the best blades, the *uagane* would form the cutting edge and the sides, almost completely enclosing the *shingane*. During the forging process, the smith would shape out the contours of the blade and tang, using a hammer and a special scraper tool.

used for the softer inner core of the blade, and another pile for those with a higher carbon content; these would create the blade's cutting edge.

Taking a selection of platelets, the armourer would then stack them around one end of an iron handle, wrap them in wet paper (to keep them together), coat the whole in a slurry of clay and powdered whetstone to act as a flux, and proceed to heat the stack until the mass of platelets fused together into a single block. Two blocks of steel were made: the heavy and hard *uagane*, tool steel to be used for the cutting edge and outer surfaces, and a softer iron *shingane* for the inner core, the latter created through greater exposure to the air, taking out most of the steel's carbon.

▶ *Produced at the beginning of the 16th century, this* katana *blade shows an* exquisite *hamon line. (Guimet Museum/CeCILL)*

▶ *The* nakago *(tang) of a* katana *inscribed by Iyonojō Muntesugu, Edo period. (Metropolitan Museum of Art/ CC-BY-2.5)*

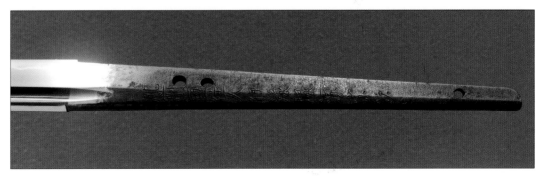

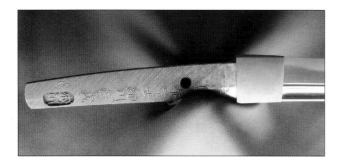

▲ *A finely crafted* wakizashi nakago *(tang) showing the* mei *(signature) and the* mekugi-ana *hole for mounting the hilt.* (Rama/CeCILL)

The blade was starting to take shape, but it still remained to be fully hardened. Here came a stage that transformed the emerging sword not only into a fully operational weapon, but also a thing of beauty. All of the blade, apart from a few millimetres of cutting edge, were coated in a paste of clay, charcoal and powdered stone, the depth of the covering being varied according to the desired level of steel hardness. Once the clay had dried, the blade was then heated up to the required temperature, before being plunged into a trough of cold water, producing rapid cooling, contraction (the blade goes through further shape changes during this process, producing the concave blade) and hardening. The parts of the sword with the thicker coating of clay, and therefore better insulated against heat, would be of softer steel than those parts uncovered or less well insulated. Smiths might also use thin intermittent strips of clay at points along the edge of the blade, creating soft chokepoints to prevent a crack in the edge propagating along the entire length of the sword.

Polishing

The sword, if on inspection it passed muster, could now be polished up and sharpened. (If there were still faults, the blade might be reheated and quenched one or two more times.) The polishing process began with abrasive polishing stones, but stepped down to the finest flakes, worked across the steel with the polisher's thumb. As the blade was polished to a lustrous shine, the contrast between hard and soft steel was revealed in beautiful, smoky lines along the side, called the *hamon*.

The nature of the *hamon*, along with other elements such as the shape of the blade and the smith's inscription on the tang, enable historians to locate the samurai sword in time and location. The cutting edge itself was sharpened up to a razor-like quality. The final act of blade-making was the fitting of a *habaki*, a sleeve of soft metal that fitted over the

intersection between blade and tang, this designed both to transmit and diffuse the vibrations of impact into the hilt, as well as to form a surface that fitted snugly into the mouth of the scabbard.

Finishing

The blade was now finished; all that was required for completion was a hilt and a *tsuba* guard piece. The *tsuba* was a flat ring of iron, often highly decorative, that sat just above the *habaki*, serving as a guard both to prevent enemy blades sliding down the sword on to the fingers, and to stop the front grip hand slipping forwards. Protective washers (*seppa*) were fitted on each side of the *tsuba*.

In terms of the hilt (*tsuka*), the Japanese swords are notable, in comparison to many European swords, in that the hilt was not a permanent fixture of the blade, but could rather be removed and replaced as required. The hilt was formed from two pieces of wood, shaped precisely to the tang and held in place by a bamboo or horn peg (*meguki*) that went through the grip sections and through a corresponding hole in the tang. The whole grip was then wrapped with a layer of soft *same*, the skin from the back of a species of ray found in the China Sea, then that in turn was typically covered with silk or leather wrapping. Diamond-shaped spaces were left in the wrapping, in which were displayed small metal ornaments called *menuki*, these serving both decorative and grip functions.

Thus, the samurai sword was completed. It was carried in a *saya* (scabbard), which was formed from lacquered magnolia wood, and which featured two small pockets, one for a utility knife known as a *kogatana*, and the other for a wooden hair-styling implement called a *kogai*.

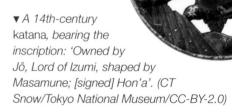

▶ *A* tsuba *(hand guard) for a* katana *shows extraordinary levels of detail, representing samurai warriors in action.* (PHGCOM/ GFDL)

▼ *A 14th-century* katana, *bearing the inscription: 'Owned by Jô, Lord of Izumi, shaped by Masamune; [signed] Hon'a'.* (CT Snow/Tokyo National Museum/CC-BY-2.0)

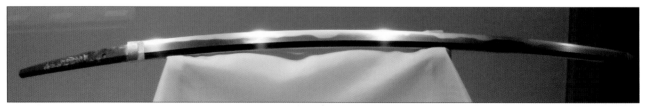

SWORD TRAINING AND FIGHTING TECHNIQUES

For all its evident beauty, the samurai sword was still a tool of violence. It was principally a slashing blade; the aim was to swing the sword fast and accurately, striking a vulnerable part of the enemy's body and then opening up the wound as the blade was drawn across its length.

The sword was almost exclusively gripped with two hands, as unlike European warriors the samurai swordsman did not carry a shield. The two-handed grip gave the swordsman exceptional levels of power, quite capable of decapitating a man with a single stroke.

SWORD DRILLS

As we have seen in the biography of Miyamoto Musashi, training in swordsmanship began young, even when the samurai child was little more than a toddler. The *Hagakure* even notes that children as young as five might practise decapitating dogs, before graduating on to real human beings in their teenage years. However, killing a hapless dog or a helpless human was very different from battling with a skilled opponent.

To gain realistic experience in the techniques of sword handling, therefore, the student had a variety of non-lethal practice options. As with today's martial artists, the samurai student spent much time drilling all the basic moves.

▲ *Although the samurai sword was primarily a slashing weapon, its hardened point was still capable of inflicting very deep penetration injuries, and could slide between gaps in armour. (Rama/CeCILL)*

Footwork had to be fast but balanced, moving in much the same way as a modern boxer, avoiding crossing the feet or loading too much weight on one foot. Musashi identifies five

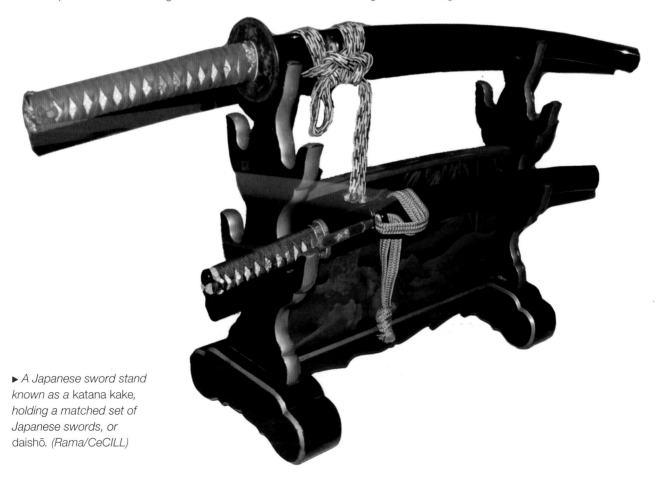

▶ *A Japanese sword stand known as a* katana kake, *holding a matched set of Japanese swords, or* daishō. *(Rama/CeCILL)*

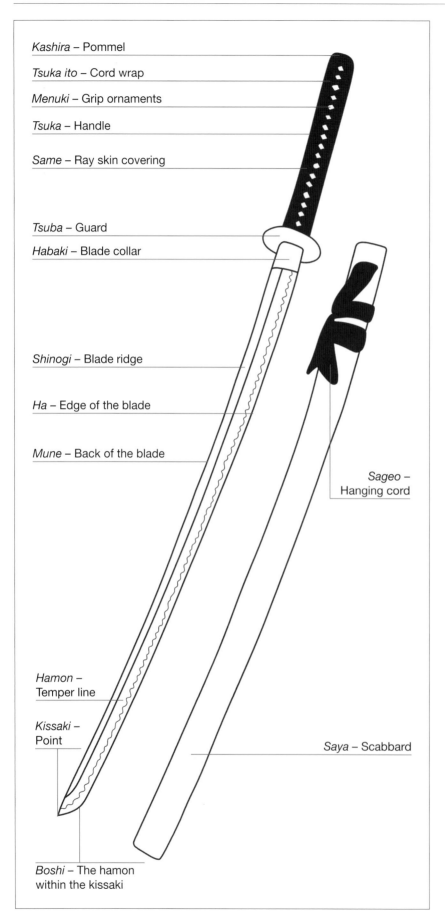

Kashira – Pommel

Tsuka ito – Cord wrap

Menuki – Grip ornaments

Tsuka – Handle

Same – Ray skin covering

Tsuba – Guard

Habaki – Blade collar

Shinogi – Blade ridge

Ha – Edge of the blade

Mune – Back of the blade

Sageo – Hanging cord

Hamon – Temper line

Kissaki – Point

Saya – Scabbard

Boshi – The hamon within the kissaki

◄ A diagram explaining the terminology behind the parts of a Japanese sword blade and its mountings. (Jarok/GFDL)

▼ Examples of various antique bokutō. Note how closely they mirror the overall shape and size of an actual 'live' blade. (Samuraiantiqueworld/CC-BY-SA-3.0)

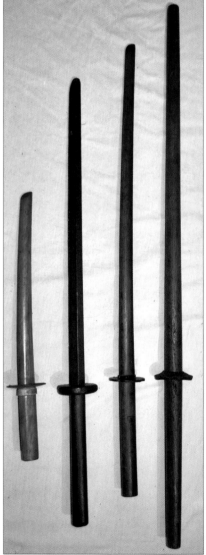

► *Having made a bold slash with his katana, this* rōnin *lunges forward, maintaining the forward momentum of the attack. (Library of Congress/ CC-PD-Mark)*

different types of guard that had to be mastered: upper position; middle position; lower position; right-hand guard; and left-hand guard, each being a position from which to protect oneself against attacks and from which attacks can be made. Indeed, Musashi enjoins the student: 'Whatever guard you adopt, do not think of it as being on guard; think of it as part of the act of killing.'[25]

STRIKE POINTS

In terms of the actual strike points for a samurai sword attack, any exposed piece of flesh was a natural target, although when facing an armour-clad opponent these might actually be few and far between. Thus, the swordsman might attack the joints between pieces of armour. Swift, snatching cuts to the opponent's arms were also useful, as they could disable the enemy's ability to fight further. More terminal blows could be delivered to the thighs (by opening up the femoral artery), abdomen and throat. If the moment presented itself, the samurai might also attempt a straight stab with the tip of the sword aimed at the opponent's heart. This technique could be useful for slipping between loosened plates of armour.

Although there was a certain degree of ritual about clashes between samurai, Musashi's work makes it clear that the swordsman had to use every tactical device at his disposal to gain superiority. These tactics were both mental and physical. Practical tips included the 'crimson foliage hit', the technique of quickly smacking down the opponent's sword with the tip of one's own sword, thereby providing a gap for exploitation. He also speaks about feinting blows to make the opponent unsteady and vulnerable, and of hitting the enemy with one's body to knock him off balance and make the distance for a decisive attack. Mentally, the samurai could use shouts, relentless pressure and intimidation to defeat the opponent psychologically, dominating his mind before going on to destroy his body.

TRAINING METHODS

Although drilling exercises brought familiarity with the physical actions of wielding a sword, there were other more combative training techniques to help the samurai develop a realistic

skill. Samurai trainees could fight each other using the wooden *bokutō* sword, cut and designed as to replicate the weight of a real sword.

An alternative to the *bokutō*, from the late 16th century, was the *shinai*, another representation of the sword, but constructed from a bundle of thin bamboo shafts, still used today in the modern sport of kendo. Both of these training weapons enabled the trainees to deliver full-power blows on each other without fatal consequences, although severe bruising and occasional fractures and concussions were often a consequence, providing the trainees with the right level of adrenaline to take the practice fight seriously.

For more experienced samurai, another training weapon was a full metal sword, albeit blunted to avoid cutting injuries. An undeflected blow from one of these weapons must have been seriously painful and genuinely dangerous, and not for the faint-hearted.

FIREARMS

The use of firearms in samurai warfare is an important counterpoint to the world of edged weapons. That firearms changed the face of warfare in Japan is undoubted. The matchlock musket, as crude as it is, was a force multiplier. It ultimately enabled a mass of relatively untrained infantry to control the battlespace, from outside the reach of a *yari* or *naginata*.

The extent of the matchlock's effective range was about 50m (55 yards) – shockingly bad by today's standards but a revolution in the 16th century. Now the samurai, regardless of his martial competence, could be cut down by a small lead ball even before he had the chance to swing his sword.

CHINESE GUNPOWDER WEAPONS

By the time firearms entered the Japanese arsenal in the 16th century, the Japanese already had some experience of gunpowder weaponry, albeit mainly on the receiving end. The Chinese and Mongols, by the 13th century, were wielding a variety of crackling and exploding gunpowder devices. Iron-shelled gunpowder bombs – known as 'thunder-crash bombs' – flung by catapults, caused consternation among the Japanese ranks in 1274, with the first Mongol attempted invasion of Japan. The terminal impact was increased by sprinkling the gunpowder charge with pieces of broken porcelain, to form a variety of shrapnel shell. Later (16th century), these bombs would even be propelled by gunpowder, via early mortar weapons. The Chinese infantry also deployed the 'fire-lance'. This was essentially a bamboo or metal tube, packed with a combustible substance that, when lit, projected a jet of blinding and blistering flame several metres in front of the operator. For good effect, the Chinese also placed small fragmented objects at the front of the tube, creating a basic projectile weapon as well as one of the earliest forms of flamethrower.

▼ *A selection of Edo period arquebus matchlock muskets. Note the very short length of the stock, which placed the priming pan very close to the face. (Rama/CC BY-SA 2.0)*

While the Japanese did not warm to the thunder-crash bombs, they did make a modest investment in the fire-lance from the mid-15th century, terming it *hiso* (fire-spear). From here, therefore, it was not too dramatic a conceptual leap to appreciate and adopt firearms when they arrived.

THE MATCHLOCK

The introduction of the matchlock arquebus in Japan can be dated fairly precisely. The first recorded incident was in 1510, when a priest named Odawara came across an imported Chinese matchlock in the town of Sakai, the priest going on to demonstrate the weapon to the local *daimyō* Hōjō Ujitsuna. Nothing appears to have come from this event, but in 1543, a small number of Portuguese traders bought high-quality arquebus ashore in a Chinese trade ship that had taken shelter on the island of Tanegashima, southern Kyushu, the weapons having been produced in a Portuguese arms plant on Goa, India. Again, these were demonstrated to the local *daimyō*, Tokitaka, but this time he saw the potential, and ordered his local smiths to make copies.

This was the beginning, and firearms began their inexhaustible spread throughout the Japanese armies, aided by the establishment of major production plants at places such as Sakai and Kunitomo, plus the enthusiastic adoption of firearms by notable *daimyō*, such as Oda Nobunaga (himself trained in gunnery) and Tokugawa Ieyasu. Both of these men, plus several other leading figures, pioneered the use of matchlocks as regimented volley weapons, ranks of arquebus-armed *ashigaru* rotating through the loading and firing procedure, resulting in a discharge of weapons

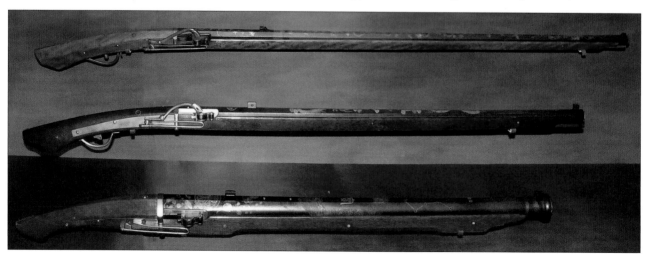

HAYAGO

Moving beyond loose powder, wadding and ball, the *hayago* was an innovation that significantly shortened loading time. Each 'cartridge' consisted of a bamboo or stick tube, containing a pre-measured quantity of powder plus wadding and ball, with multiple cartridges stored in a *hayago doran* cartridge box. To use a *hayago*, the gunner would tear off the paper seal from one end, and tip the gunpowder charge down the barrel. Then, using his ramrod, he would push the ball and wadding out from the tube and directly into the barrel, ramming them down while either storing or discarding the now-empty tube.

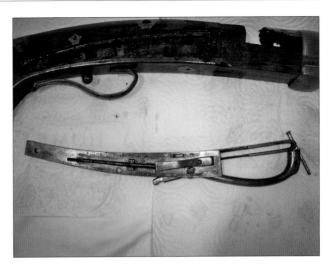

▲ *This dismantled Japanese matchlock illustrates the fundamental mechanical simplicity of the operating mechanism. (Samuraiantiqueworld/CC-BY-SA-3.0)*

▼ *Three views of a Japanese matchlock pistol, the bronze barrel engraved with golden and silver inlays of flying birds and grass. (Worldantiques/CC-BY-SA-3.0)*

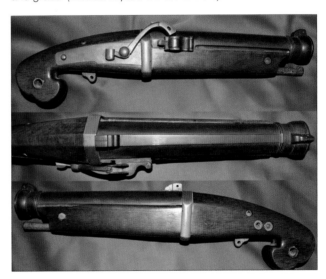

approximately every five seconds, depending on various factors (see below).

The matchlocks used in Japan came in various shapes and sizes. The vast majority were weapons that could be fired from the shoulder in a standing position, typically firing musket balls in the region of 8–9mm in calibre. In fact, an early innovation in Japanese firearm production was to produce standardised bore sizes, unlike in medieval Europe, where musket bores could vary in diameter from weapon to weapon. Standardising the calibre was an important step not only because it facilitated a level of mass production, but also because it simplified logistics on the campaign and the battlefield; an army could have a single common ammunition supply, or could mould new musket balls, knowing that they could be used by every weapon.

The effective range of these weapons was about 30–50m (33–55 yards), but there are images showing far larger and heavier matchlocks, almost like mini cannon, that reputedly could reach out to approximately 300m (328 yards). The great size and weight of these firearms meant that they could not be fired from the shoulder; the illustrations depict the gunner firing a weapon from a sitting position, the lower stock of the gun draped across his lap and the butt pressed up against sandbags, to absorb what would evidently be hefty recoil. The calibre of these weapons could be nearly an inch.

MECHANISM AND FIRING PROCEDURE

The Portuguese model of arquebus, which became dominant in the Japanese armouries, was based around a simple and reliable mechanism. The weapon was muzzle-loading. The loading procedure began with the gunner upending the weapon, butt on the ground, and tipping a measured quantity of loose powder down the barrel. Once this was done, a musket ball and paper wadding were inserted into the muzzle and compacted down on to the charge using a ramrod. The ramrods were obviously highly critical parts of the gunner's kit, and a broken ramrod could render a weapon non-functional. For this reason, the *teppo ko gashira* – the junior officer in charge of an arquebus squad – himself always carried a spare

ramrod, held inside a bamboo case. Next, the gunner held the weapon level in front of him, and deposited, from a special flask, a small amount of priming powder into the priming pan, holding the powder in place by swinging a hinged priming pan lid into place.

Once the gun was loaded, it had to be made ready to fire. The Japanese arquebus was a matchlock weapon: a smouldering length of slow-match was attached to a thin spring-loaded metal arm, what was called a 'serpentine' in Europe but a *hibasami* in Japan. The upper end of the arm held the smouldering match, which was blown, fanned or twirled in the air to get the heat up. The arm was cocked by pulling it back against a spring, a trigger beneath the stock acting as the serpentine release.

When the moment to fire had come, the gunner would

▲ *Japanese re-enactors fire a volley of matchlock firearms. The smoke produced by dozens of shooters would have been choking. (CC-BY-SA-4.0)*

THE PARTS OF A JAPANESE MATCHLOCK

- *shiba-hikigane* – butt protector
- *hikigane* – trigger
- *karakuri* – lock
- *jiita* – plate
- *yuojintetsu* – trigger guard
- *biyu* – rivet
- *hinawa toushi ana* – hole for the matchcord
- *hajiki gane* – spring
- *dugane* – stock ring
- *hibasami* – hammer arm
- *amaoi* – barrel protector
- *hibuta* – pan cover
- *hizara* – pan tray
- *dai* – stock
- *tsutsu* – barrel
- *moto maete* – rear sight
- *udenuki* – sling hole
- *naka maete* – middle sight
- *mekugi ana* – pin hole
- *saki maete* – front sight
- *karuka* – ramrod
- *suguchi* – muzzle

swing the pan cover back to expose the priming powder, shoulder the gun and point it in the right direction using the weapon's simple blade front sight and rear notch, then on the command pull the trigger. This released the serpentine, which now dropped the smouldering match on to the priming powder; when this powder ignited, a hot flame shot down the vent hole between pan and chamber, igniting the powder in the chamber and firing the weapon.

CAPABILITIES

Compared to rifled weapons – which because of subsequent isolationism never entered the Japanese arsenal until the 19th century – the smoothbore matchlocks were not accurate weapons. Hence, as the Europeans discovered, the best way to use the matchlock was as part of a mass volley, the volume of fire compensating for individual inaccuracies. Yet this is not to say that the Japanese muskets were hopelessly inaccurate in trained hands. Respected historian of the samurai Stephen Turnbull explains, in his recommended work *The Samurai Sourcebook*, how modern trials of arquebus accuracy have produced some notable results.[26] Firing at human-shaped targets at ranges of 30m (33 yards) and 50m (55 yards), five shots at each range, the test gunners (admittedly highly trained personnel) hit the 30m (33-yard) targets in the chest area with all five shots. At 50m (55 yards), the number of hits to the chest area dropped to just one in five, but there were strikes on other parts of the target body; even if these hits had not been fatal, they could have removed the enemy soldier from the fight.

▲ *A samurai re-enactor begins the process of reloading his arquebus. Note the length of match that he has in his left hand. (Corpse Reviver/CC-BY-SA-3.0)*

▲ *A fur-covered arrow quiver from the Edo period. Note the wooden spool for holding a bow string. (Sailko/Tokyo National Museum / CC-BY-SA-3.0)*

Furthermore, during the trials the shots were fired against different target materials to test the penetration capabilities: 24mm and 48mm wooden boards were used, and 1mm and 2mm iron plate. At 30m (33 yards) all of these targets were pierced through, and at 50m (55 yards) the 24mm wooden board and 1mm iron plate were cleanly penetrated; the 48mm board and 2mm iron plate were not punched through, but the ball went three-quarters of the way through the board and dented and lodged in the iron plate. Thus, in terms of both accuracy and penetration – bearing in mind that the wooden boards and armour plate either represented or exceeded the resistance of Japanese body armour – the matchlock musket created a definite zone of lethality up to 50m (55 yards) away from the muzzle.

It was likely for this reason that from the 16th century we see a shift in samurai battlefield tactics. Prior to the advent of firearms, it was common for the samurai to lead from the front in battle, standing out ahead of the *ashigaru* or peasant soldiers, issuing defiant proclamations to their enemy then fighting the opposing samurai before opening up the battle to the infantry behind. As it became increasingly lethal to put oneself in front of the massed ranks of *ashigaru* muskets, the battles came to be led by exchanges of musket and archery fire, with the samurai only entering the combat once the distance weapons had begun to exert their effect.

Although the musket undoubtedly had a transformative effect on Japanese warfare, there were inherent limitations to the matchlock that require compensation from other weapons systems. Theoretically, it should have taken about 15 seconds for a well-trained gunner to perform the full cycle of loading and firing, resulting in a rate of fire of about 4rpm. However, the fouling inherent in black-powder muskets would progressively reduce the rate of fire as more rounds were put down the barrel. There were also the problems of damp or wet weather affecting the combustion of the gunpowder or the burning of the match. There were some measures to improve the weatherproofing of the match, including boiling the fuse in a mixture of gallnut and tooth-blackening powder, and storing it in a wrapped waxed cloth,[27] but significant rainfall could render ranks of gunners almost silent. Such effects, combined with the natural friction of performing complex physical actions during battle, meant that sustaining rates of fire at full pace was problematic, if not impossible. For this reason, archers complemented muskets on the field of battle. Archers were more accurate, had greater effective range and could maintain fire regardless of the weather. It took years of practice to produce a competent archer, however, but only days to train an *ashigaru* to put a musket ball into massed enemy troops. To a large extent, the matchlock musket ushered in the age of infantry-formation warfare in Japan.

CHAPTER SIX

SAMURAI ON CAMPAIGN

Samurai campaigning has to be viewed through the prism of Japan's deeply feudal social structure. Feudalism operates through a cascading authority, stemming (in the Japanese context) from the shogun or emperor at the very top, down to the lowest agricultural peasant at the very bottom. Each person in society owed his or her fealty to those above, and while the world largely went on to reject feudalism as an organising structure, it did have its advantages when the time came to call society to arms.

▶ *A 19th-century colour woodblock print shows samurai warriors on the march, illustrating some of the hierarchical and organisational principles at play. (Heritage Image Partnership Ltd / Alamy)*

SOCIAL RANKS AND MOBILISATION

Japanese society in the age of the samurai was highly stratified socially and materially. Every person, and every warrior, had to understand and commit to his or her place in this hierarchy. The social structures were especially visible during times of war, when an army was called together and organised for the forthcoming campaign.

DAIMYŌ

The social ranks of Japan during periods of study were extremely complex, with many fine grades of distinction even within what we perceive to be a single class strata. The pivotal figure when the call-to-arms came was the *daimyō*, who now had to turn a largely part-time military resource into a full-time fighting army.

The *daimyō* himself brought some personal muscle to the fight. In the *Kōyō Gunkan*, a 20-scroll chronicle of the Takeda family of Kai Province, the composition of the Takeda army in 1573 is given, including a description of the *hatamoto shoyakunin,* those who directly attended the lord. In total, the *daimyō* had a personal force of some 884 individuals performing a busy spectrum of functions. In addition to

personal bodyguard troops, the entourage also included pages, storeroom managers, banner bearers, finance commissioners, kitchen staff, secretaries, personal attendants, horse vets and, for the *daimyō*'s personal entertainment, an actor.

SAMURAI

The *daimyō*'s primary tool of mobilisation was his samurai, the elite tier of society in whose hands lay much of the concentration of wealth and power. Through the allocation of *koku* to the samurai, which in turn governed how many warriors he could support (and who therefore owed their fealty to him), the samurai was the critical link between the *daimyō* and the field army. We need to acknowledge some of

▼ *A portrait of Uesugi Kenshin, one of the great samurai generals. In this image, note his traditional bearskin boots. (Utagawa Yoshitora/CC-PD-Mark)*

▼ *A letter from the Mongol leader Kublai Khan to Japan in 1266, threatening the country with invasion if it did not submit to his will. (CC-PD-Mark)*

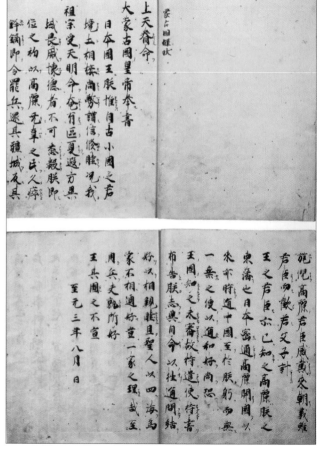

▲ *A group of samurai warriors marching in a procession during the Jidai Matsuri Festival of Ages in Kyoto, Japan. (Photo Japan/Alamy)*

the subtleties within the system, however. For example, we should not regard the samurai themselves as one homogenous elite mass. The wealth and therefore status of individual samurai could vary quite considerably, ranging from men with tens of thousands of *koku* down to samurai who themselves worked as part-time farmers to make ends meet. Other factors, such as the family from which the samurai came and the military service he had performed, could all have a bearing on his status, although the samurai remained an authoritative class. Each samurai would also have two personal retainers/followers, these supporting the samurai with both high and low functions, from guiding his personal grooming through to accompanying him into battle.

Note that just the fact of being a samurai did not ensure that you automatically took an influential position of leadership in the warring army. The Natori-ryu scrolls devote some space to the topic of *Senshi no ho*, 'The Way of Selecting Samurai'. An interesting opening passage states that it is useful to select poor samurai for high-risk assaults, as proving themselves in battle was a good way to improve social standing, therefore they would be highly motivated to throw themselves into the attack. Young and healthy samurai should be used as scouts, while men particularly noted for bravery could be used 'to attack castle gates, break fences, backfill moats and other similar tasks', although what is similar about these tasks is open to question. For samurai of intellect and good language skills, the recommendation is to keep them out of the action and use them instead for morale-building (delivering encouraging messages) and for work as *kancho*

(spies). 'Cowards', on the other hand, or those who exhibited 'timidity', could be sidelined as gate keepers, fire watchers and leading night security patrols.

ASHIGARU

The *ashigaru* are another interesting case in the Japanese feudal model, as they became far more than mere foot-sloggers at the lowest ranks. As the influence of the *ashigaru* rose during the 16th century, gradually their status increased until they de facto stepped on to the lowest rungs of the samurai hierarchy. This advancement was accentuated from 1587, when Toyotomi Hideyoshi – himself risen from the ranks of the *ashigaru* – sought to strengthen his control of Japan and solidify the social hierarchy by implementing a *katanagatari* (sword hunt), banning the peasantry from keeping weapons.

The peasant class historically made up the numbers on the battlefield, but they also represented a potential force that could be turned against him by a rebel *daimyō*. Hideyoshi's armies went out across the country, confiscating weaponry from the poorest of society. This had the effect, however, of visibly raising the status of the armed *ashigaru*, who now effectively took membership of the warrior class. Thus it was that the men who commanded large *ashigaru* units, called *ashigaru-taisho*, often became prestigious figures within Japanese society, equal to all but the highest ranks of pure-blood samurai.

The growth of the *ashigaru* by no means meant that the peasantry of Japan became exempt from military service in times of war. Peasants and farmers would still be called up, although primarily in support role functions, assisting in logistics, the construction of field fortifications and care for livestock and horses.

▼ *A force of* ashigaru *emplace themselves behind wicker barricades, ready to conduct a defence with their arquebuses. (PD-Japan)*

AN ARMY READY

During times of conflict or turmoil, all sectors of Japanese society would be ready for war at short notice. Samurai retainers kept their master's arms and armour in perfect order, and it is said that many *ashigaru* working in the fields would actually have spears stuck into the ground nearby, and campaign kit piled and ready.

MUSTERING

In all but the most urgent instances, the army would be raised over a period of several days, the *daimyō* sending out messages to the samurai, who in turn would send out their own messages to the *ashigaru* and others, telling them to be ready for moving out at the sound of a drum, bell or *jinkai* ('war shell') – a large conch shell fitted with a mouthpiece and used as a trumpet. (Note that the *jinkai* had further military instructional functions, used for tasks such as controlling the rhythm of marching or for sending battlefield commands for units to move, advance, retreat etc.) When the instrument sounded, in the early morning, all the samurai and *ashigaru* would make their way to a muster point, where there would be a roll call and orders given.

If the army had to be mustered immediately with little prior warning, the *daimyō* would rely upon fast horse-mounted messengers, but also a chain of signal fires that could transmit visual signals from station to station at great speed. It was said that in the Takeda territories a message could be sent from Sutama to the capital Kofu, a distance of 160km (100 miles), in less than two hours.[28]

PRE-MARCH RITUALS

In such a religious age, it should not be surprising that there was much ceremony and ritual that accompanied the formation of an army and its march off to war. Prayers would first be spoken by priests, invoking the *kami* to bless the army in its endeavours. The principal *kami* invoked was Hachiman Dai Bosatsu, the god of archery and war and the protector over Japan, the divine incarnation of the Emperor Ōjin. There would be many other acts of divination and prayer across the strata of the army, each warrior and group attempting to access the good fortune that would bring victory and hopefully survival.

Those who were sensitive to such things knew how to spot good and bad omens in the preparations. For example, if the *daimyō*'s horse turned its nose to face in the direction of the enemy, this was viewed positively, whereas it was an ill omen if it turned away from the enemy.[29] The warriors also had to keep away from supposedly 'polluting' influences on

▼ *The scale of military mobilisation is suggested by this image of the Siege of Ulsan (1598). The attacking forces totalled about 50,000 men. (PD-Japan)*

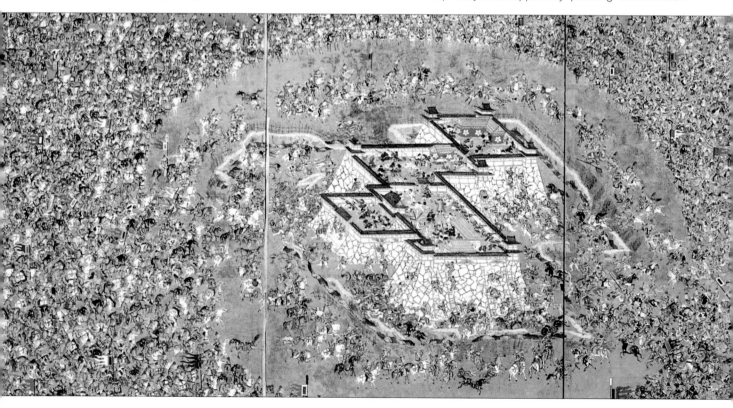

SIGNAL FIRES

The Japanese used signal fires to good effect during the Sengoku *jidai*. At their most basic, these were large fires pre-built on high ground, in clear line of sight of the next fire station in the line. In addition to fires, the stations might also have firework-type flares, giving extra elevation to the message. The most sophisticated devices, however, were the *noroshi* (lit. 'fox smoke') towers. At first glance, these had an appearance somewhat akin to a European trebuchet, with an open three-storey wooden tower topped by a very long pivoting beam, holding a large metal brazier at one end. The brazier, lowered down to ground level, was filled with the combustible materials in readiness. At times of sudden emergency, the fire was lit and the brazier then pivoted up to its maximum elevation, sending a prominent signal to the next station, whose crew would then light their own fire, and so on.

For a further refinement of instruction, note that the colour of the fire could be controlled to a certain degree by adding the following substances:

- ■ saltpetre – white fire
- ■ sulphur – yellow fire
- ■ camphor – blue fire
- ■ charcoal – black fire
- ■ moxa (dried mugwort) – red fire

During night-time hours, the main signal element would be the flames, while in the daylight smoke would be preferred. The signal fires would also be monitored by the occupants of military watchtowers. It was recommended that the watchtower crews physically mark out the direction of the *noroshi* or signal fires, so that they would know which way they should be looking. They could define the direction either through carving markings on to the wooden posts of the watchtower or by making direction markers using bamboo posts and rope.

▲ *Samurai armour had undoubted utility in battle, but on campaign it could be a personal logistical burden. (Didier ZYLBERYNG/ Alamy)*

the approach to war, such as menstruating or post-partum women or dead bodies. According to Taoist traditions, there were also certain dates of the year on which it was unlucky to initiate a military campaign. These were:

- ■ spring – 7th, 14th, 21st days
- ■ summer – 8th, 16th, 24th days
- ■ autumn – 9th, 18th, 27th days
- ■ winter – 10th, 21st, 30th days.[30]

If all the heavenly symbols and portents appeared to be configured appropriately, the army's elite, set in a large curtained mobile headquarters known as a *maku*, would then eat a farewell meal, its three dishes – dried chestnuts, kelp

▶ *A full set of samurai* kusari gusoku *or chain armour, from the Edo period. (Samuraiantique-world/CC-BY-SA-3.0)*

and abalone – set by tradition. The food was washed down by sake served inside three stacked cups, the number three being a propitious one in Japanese culture.

CODES OF DISCIPLINE

Any Japanese army about to embark on a campaign also had to be versed in the rules and regulations that would govern their expedition. A large army was a sprawling social entity, containing all manner of classes, attitudes, experience and expectations, and commanders had to enforce strict guidelines about the behaviours that would be encouraged and those that would be punished, sometimes mortally so.

In the *Scroll of Heaven* from the Natori-ryu, there is a section entitled 'Announcements to make to all samurai before marching'. The author acknowledges that the dictums vary between clans and generals, but they nevertheless provide fascinating insight into the pre-march set-up. The key point emphasised is that all soldiers on the march, regardless of their social rank, maintain good order, keep row formations and show quick obedience to commands from the general. There follows an extended discussion of what to do if people were sick either prior to embarking on the campaign or during the march itself. Respect for the suffering is apparent; there does not seem to be any of the dismissive attitude towards casualties often found in European warfare. For those who become ill, it was recommended that they be left in a residence along the route of the march, in the company of someone who would care for them and hopefully help restore them to health. The author recognised that few of the warlike samurai would volunteer for the unglamorous, and potentially dangerous (in the case of infectious diseases), duty of carer, hence advocated falling back on the process of *atarikuji*, the drawing of lots, specifically among five men from the casualty's unit. Should the sick person die, it was imperative that he be given a proper funeral, regardless of the exigencies of the campaign. The text notes that: 'Not giving the dead a proper burial should be considered a sin as serious as abandoning a friend.'[31]

PILLAGING

The writer then lays down the rules for pillaging. In general, the samurai army was governed by codes of respect for the people in the territories through which they passed, although as we shall see in the next chapter, there were many instances where propriety gave way to barbarity. There was to be no pillaging unless specifically authorised by the commanders, and when it was authorised, the order in which units undertook the pillaging might be governed by lot. Pillaging generally took place during campaigns of extended duration and distance, when food transported from the point of origin was no longer sufficient to sustain the army. The Natori-ryu gives a descending order of priority for which materials should be collected if pillaging is authorised: first military equipment and weapons; second, food; third, gold and silver.

BEHAVIOUR AND PUNISHMENT

Each person on the march would be assigned a specific location in the march formation, and the *Scroll of Heaven* cautions the samurai about any arguments over allocated positions, enjoining the warriors to take up their place without dispute. The author makes a general point that all warriors, high and low, should refrain from any manner of brawling or fighting, explaining that 'these fights stem from personal grudges', and therefore have no place within the higher purpose of the army.

Masuzumi also includes in the *Scroll of Heaven* a long list of *batsuho* (Codes for Punishment), a strict set of penal regulations under which all the army would operate. These were separated into three sections: *juzai* (serious charges), for which the penalty was invariably death; *chuzai* (mid-level charges), which brought a formal court-martial; and *gezai* (low-level charges), which involved informal investigation and the imposition of minor fines.

A selection of the *juzai* illustrate some of the key behaviours that would not be tolerated under any circumstances; there is a note at the end of the section stating that anyone committing these transgressions should be 'killed without discussion':

▶ *The samurai commander Saigō Takamori (1828–77) sits surrounded by his officers during the Satsuma Rebellion. (CC-PD-Mark)*

- Making an attack ahead of one's unit against the commander's orders. (This illustrates how by the 17th century the age of a brash samurai making a spirited unilateral attack was largely over.)
- Feigning illness to get out of fighting.
- Being indiscreet when talking about tactics with strangers.
- Entering or exiting a battle camp from anywhere except the main gate.
- Committing theft from allied soldiers during battle.
- Raping or kidnapping local women.
- Abandoning comrades and fleeing the battlefield during action.
- Inadvertently alerting the enemy by talking loudly or indiscreetly while in concealed positions.

Although some of these capital offences would have made sense even in 20th-century armies, others – such as the procedures for entering and exiting camp – seem harsh, although they reflect the critical role of security during campaigns. It has to be remembered that the wars of Japan were largely internal civil conflicts, therefore it could be extremely difficult to separate friend from foe on either visual or linguistic levels, so security procedures had to be extremely tight.

The *chuzai,* or mid-level, charges, bring their own set of surprises to modern eyes. Samurai and *ashigaru* could be charged, sometimes with good reason, for simple errors in competence, such as failing to report important information in a timely fashion, wandering away from guard duty, and making false statements of fact. There are other offences that are severe and which we might expect to be placed in the *juzai* category, including deliberate arson or murder of men and women in enemy territory, or killing servants 'without good reason'.

The *gezai,* or low-level, offences are merely a litany of poor behaviour, idleness and stupidity. Among the infractions are gossipy talk, 'making a fuss without good reason', making unnecessary noise, neglecting the practice of their martial skills and criticising their commander's orders. One offence that particularly stands out is that of a warrior carrying weapons or armour that exceeded his social status; in the feudal Japanese mind, it was important that everyone knew his place.

One common thread in Japanese military codes of discipline are measures to prevent disorder, both physical and social. Such is seen in a list of regulations issued by Tokugawa Ieyasu in 1590, as his army set up camp during the siege of Odara Castle. Some of the stipulations mirror those already given above, such as punishments for samurai who advance too far forwards to make a name for themselves (notably, Ieyasu states that not only will the samurai be punished, but also his family), and for those who march in a disorderly fashion, without the proper discipline. Ieyasu is also clear that any violence or intimidation towards local tradespeople was absolutely forbidden; transgressors would receive an immediate death sentence.

▲ A re-creation of an armoured samurai riding a horse, showing contemporary horse armour. Many samurai would campaign on foot, however. (tiseb/C-BY-2.0)

▼ A Japanese Edo period woodblock print shows a samurai putting on his dō, tying his shoulder straps. (Ayakawa Kyuukei/CC-PD-Mark)

THE MARCHING ARMY

After the performance of the pre-march rituals, the moment came for the army to set off on its campaign. The *daimyō* would stand before the massed array, clutching a war fan and shout *Ei!* (Glory!), to which the soldiers would reply *Oh!* (Yes). Next, a multitude of banners and standards would be unfurled, the commander would mount his horse, and the army would set off.

ORDER OF MARCH

The samurai army on the march was a leviathan of humanity, numbering anywhere from a few thousand men up to tens of thousands. It was not a disordered mass; its composition and the order in which units took their place in the column was strictly regimented. The order would vary internally according to the commander and the campaign, but some general principles can be determined based on extant records, such as the scrolls of the Natori-ryu and the *Taikoki*, a biography of Toyotomi Hideyoshi written in the first half of the 17th century.

At the head of the marching column would be carried the flags and standards of the army, accompanied by the *samurai-daishō* (samurai commanders).

Next would come the principal combat troops: first the *yumi-teppo* (musketeers and archers) along with the *ashigaru-daishō* (leader of the foot soldiers), then those armed with *naginata* or *yari*, along with large numbers of mounted and dismounted samurai. Following these warriors would be the musicians equipped with *oshidaiko* (marching drums), conch-shell trumpets and gongs. Their important role would be to keep time for the marching soldiers, and musically transfer commands to the troops, such as stoppages in responses to sudden attacks. (Masuzumi noted that it was important for all troops to stay as quiet as possible while marching, so that they could hear the musical instruments.)

Following the musicians would be the commanding general and his bodyguard and entourage, his position in the column marked by the *umajirushi* (general's battle standard). Finally, at the rear of the march was a general mass of soldiery, including more dismounted and mounted samurai and their retainers, as well as various messengers and logistics troops.

PACE OF MARCH AND TERRAIN CHALLENGES

In the *Scroll of Heaven*, it was recommended that marching began at around 5–7am every morning and was maintained until about 1–3pm, although the author acknowledges that this routine could vary significantly depending on the campaign. He also stipulates that the ideal daily marching distance is 5–6 *ri*; one *ri* is just under 4km (2.5 miles), so the expectation is that the army could achieve up to 24km (15 miles) per day, a not-unreasonable figure given that the army was marching for up to ten hours a day. It was imperative that anything that could disrupt the steady pace of march, such as a sick person or a disobedient and disruptive horse, was quickly removed from the ranks to the side of the road.

Japan is by its nature an extremely mountainous country,

▼ *A samurai war council makes plans before the Battle of Yamazaki in 1582. Note the curtains of the* maku *surrounding the group. (Fujiarts/CC-PD-Mark)*

WAR FANS

Japanese war fans are, to Western eyes, a very curious, almost comical, subset of the samurai arsenal. They were of various types, and they served a surprisingly broad array of purposes. One of the most innocuous types was the *gunsen*, made with wooden or metal spokes and covered with lacquered paper, which was used by men as well as women simply for keeping cool under the hot Japanese sun. A more aggressive variety was the *tessen*, which was made purely of iron plates. When folded, the heavy *tessen* could function as a form of club or could be thrown at an enemy. When the fan was open, it served as an improvised shield to deflect arrows and sword blows, and the upper edge of the fan could also be used as a slashing tool. *Tessen* were particularly useful as easy to conceal objects for a samurai to carry into places where conventional weapons were prohibited.

Of similar function to the *tessen* was the *gunbai*. This was a non-collapsible paddle-type fan made of solid iron or solid wood, and was a formidable if aesthetically pleasing object. The skill of war fan combat was known as *tessenjutsu*. Not only were war fans used for occasional fighting, but they were also used by commanders as signalling devices.

▲ *A* tessen *(iron fan) on display in Iwakuni Castle illustrates how very solid and club-like these instruments could be. (Mkill / PD-Self)*

▶ *Two high-quality Japanese* gunsen *war fans from the 14th (top) and 18th centuries. These were used mostly for simply staying cool. (Шнапс/CC-BY-SA-3.0)*

▶ *Toyotomi Hideyoshi (seated) and Kuroda Yoshitaka, his chief strategic advisor, make campaign plans using a basic map. (Museum of Fine Arts/CC-PD-Mark)*

TYPES OF TROOPS

Samurai armies contained some very distinctive positions in their ranks, especially if we include the mass of retainers and assistants, virtually an army within an army. The following is a selection of some distinctive examples, with their key roles:

- *Teppo ashigaru kogashira* (*ashigaru* musket sergeant) – In charge of units of musketeers, conducting the firing process with his baton, maintaining correct firing procedure and weapon handling, and monitoring ammunition consumption.
- *Yumi ashigaru kogashira* (bowman sergeant) – Similar duties to the *teppo ashigaru kogashira*, but specifically relating to the *ashigaru* archers.
- *Mochiyari katsugi* (spear-carrying servant) – Maintaining the condition and availability of a *yari* or *naginata* for a samurai master, and repairing the weapon following battle damage or acquiring a new one after its loss.
- *Hatasashi umajirushi mochi* (commander's standard bearer) – Carrying the commander's standard in a shaft attached to a leather support holder worn around the waist. It is noted in the *Zōhyō Monogatari* (The Foot Soldier's Tales), written in the late 17th century, that the *hatasashi umajirushi mochi* would go on to the battlefield if necessary and join in the fight, striking the enemy with the long shaft of the standard.
- *Mochizutsu* (musket-carrying servant) – This individual carried a musket and its ammunition for a samurai, the musket either being worn, via a sling, on the shoulder or, in the case of very large muskets, on the back, and with the cartridge box draped around the neck.
- *Zoritori* (sandal-carrying servant) – The *zoritori* did indeed carry his master's sandals, but many other personal effects besides, and he acted in much the same way as a modern batman to an officer. The *zoritori* attached to a great lord was a very important figure, with much influence over the lord's day-to-day activities.
- *Hasamibako mochi* (box-carrying servant) – Responsible for carrying his master's travelling box or trunk, which contained many of the samurai's personal possessions and spare equipment. Should any of the contents be damaged, the *hasamibako mochi* would make or arrange repairs.

laced with many rivers and streams, and subject to extremes of weather in both the summer and the winter months. The physical conditions of the march, therefore, could have a profound effect upon the pace and the distance achieved by an army on the move. Scouts moving out ahead of the army would reconnoitre difficult terrain to find the best pass through for the advancing troops. Such information might also be gleaned from local guides and spies.

Yet in all but the most treacherous conditions, the samurai army would still be able to maintain a decent degree of momentum, based on their physical toughness and their familiarity with Japan's landscape. For example, one technique for negotiating heavy snow was to have all mounted troops dismount, and then place the horses in front of the warriors, the heavy animals serving to compact the snow for human footfall. Nor were rivers insurmountable

◀ *The emblem (mon) of the Toyotomi clan, the clan of the legendary Toyotomi Hideyoshi. (Zagyoso/ PD-user)*

obstacles. In contrast to many European military traditions, the Japanese soldiers of the past were positively encouraged to learn to swim, and also to acclimatise their horses with the experience of swimming. Incredibly, many samurai trained themselves to swim even while wearing their full suit of armour, and with their weapons held above their heads to keep them dry. If the warrior, or his retainers, were not strong swimmers they could wear various types of buoyancy aid to help them to the other side. These included cork floats strapped around the torso, pieces of wood wedged under the armpits or animal skins. Mounted troops would typically dismount when they reached a river and allow their grooms to swim across the river with the horse, ideally with one man either side of the animal holding the reins. There were recorded instances, however, where samurai made an early form of amphibious combat crossing, sitting upon the horse's back and firing arrows as they came within range.

SCOUTS AND SECURITY

Security was a major concern for a samurai on the move. Despite some of the formalities of Japanese warfare, ambushes and spying were common, the former becoming increasingly so during the age of firearms. For this reason, *monomi* (scouts) were deployed in large numbers ahead of and surrounding the Japanese army. The instructions of the Natori-ryu are clear:

Never let your guard down and frequently send out *monomi* scouts, especially in enemy territory where you are not familiar with the landscape. Also use guides, but remember that those guides may be spies for the enemy and may intend to lead you into a disadvantageous position. Sometimes it is best to divide your men into two and take two different routes when marching. In this case use flags as signals between the two forces. If darkness falls and it is difficult to see these signal flags, use fire to communicate. This is done in order to rejoin forces and make camp.[32]

Scout formations could range in size from several hundred warriors – making what we would probably call today a 'reconnaissance in force' – down to just one or two individuals conducting covert spying. The *monomi* unit would usually be composed of *kachi-gashira* (captains of warriors on foot), as these individuals would have both combat experience and better judgement when it came to collecting intelligence, such as accurately judging the size of enemy forces. Masazumi states that: 'Basically, every samurai should know the way of *monomi* scouting.' The scouts were not merely required to go out and observe the enemy, but also to make judgements about how the enemy would deploy themselves tactically, and how the allies could respond to the threat.

The *monomi* would pay special attention to those parts of the landscape in which ambushing enemy forces might easily be able to conceal themselves, such as mountain passes, valleys, thick woodland, riverbanks, narrow paths surrounded by foliage, and large rice fields. If they spotted enemy forces, they would have to make accurate assessments of their size, strength and combat capability. Looking again at the writings of the Natori-ryu, the modern reader can be struck by the sophistication of advice given to the scouts, advice that will be readily used by modern reconnaissance troops, albeit with some cultural translation. For example, when observing an enemy army on the march, the scout should estimate that each individual mounted warrior occupied 1 *ken* of physical space – an individual *ken* equates to 1.8m (5ft 10in) – the same distance that is occupied by two soldiers on foot. If the army were marching in double column, then each *cho* (109m or 119 yards) would contain roughly 120 mounted troops or 240 foot warriors. The scouts were also instructed to think carefully about how their physical position might affect their estimations of enemy strength. When observing from an elevated position, for example, numbers might appear greater than when observing the same force from ground level. Scouts also had to be adept at reading the signs of intended enemy movement. If the enemy himself sent out a greater frequency of scouts, while also massing *ashigaru* troops at the front of his formation, that would likely indicate an intention to make an offensive action.

Once the scout troops had their information, they would relay it back to

▲ *A set of antique samurai armour, considered to be the armour of Ashikaga Takauji. (AlkaliSoaps/Metropolitan Museum of Art/CC-BY-2.0)*

▼ *A Japanese* jinkai *(conch shell trumpet). The pitch of the sound can be changed be altering the tension in the lips. (Samuraiantiqueworld/CC-BY-SA-3.0)*

the army commanders. There were various options for doing this. Messengers might be sent on fast horses or, if the security arrangements allowed it, they may use signal fires or other visual devices. There were even prearranged sequences of horse-riding movements, which when performed would give basic information to a distant observer, the use of the mount increasing the range of the communication by several hundred metres.

HORSES AND GROOMS

The desired characteristics of horses in Japanese samurai armies contrast somewhat with those of the contemporary European theatre. While European cavalry sought out horses of height, speed and power (at least for battlefield use), Japanese mounted troops preferred the short but stocky Kiso horses, which were only in the region of 120–140cm (4ft–4ft 8in) in height at the shoulder. The mountainous terrain of Japan meant that the ideal military horse had a low centre of gravity and much traction from negotiating precipitous landscapes. These characteristics meant that the Japanese horses had limited, but still serviceable, speed on the battlefield, although this became less important as

dismounted warfare became the norm from the 16th century.

The chief men in charge of a horse were the samurai's two grooms, or *umatori*. A fascinating insight into their roles and practical daily duties is given in the *Zōhyō Monogatari*. The two accounts of the fictitious *umatori,* by 'Kinroku' and 'Toroku', begin by listing the large array of equestrian equipment associated with the warhorse, equipment they have both to maintain and utilise. The equipment included:

- a horse ladle (an instrument used for washing the animal)
- the *hananeji* 'nose twister'
- headgear and bridle
- saddle-girth (used for keeping the saddle in place when riding)
- martingale (straps that prevent the horse from raising its head too high)

Samurai *kura no koto* (saddles) were made of two pieces of curved wood with the saddle seat in between. The wood featured *tegata* handholds cut into their edges, to give grip during mounting and dismounting. The Natori-ryu text explains the origins of this feature in the Heiji Rebellion of

▼ *A spear-armed samurai warrior watches a ship burn offshore. Ships were often used as troop transports along the coast or to offshore islands. (Chronicle/Alamy)*

▼ *The* daimyō *Kanamori Shigeyori riding into action on his fine horse. Japan adopted the stirrup in the 5th century, a technology that changed mounted combat. (CC-PD-Mark)*

▲ *A Japanese Edo period woodblock print, an illustration from the famous* Zōhyō Monogatari, *shows two* ashigaru *grooms watering a horse. (PD-Japan)*

1160, when warrior Minamoto no Tomonaga found himself in freezing winter conditions that made it difficult for him for grip his saddle to mount his horse. Acting on the suggestion of samurai Akugenta Yoshihara, Kamata Masakiyo assisted Tomonaga by using his sword to slice two handholds into the saddle, and the utility of this modification apparently stuck with the Japanese army.

The *Zōhyō Monogatari* account continues by explaining how the groom should load the horse with supplies, illustrating the role of every horse in basic logistics:

> Load the horse with the *Mentsu*, which is a wooden container for rice on the left saddle ring, while the small musket and the flag-holding cylinder go on the right side of the ring. On each of the rear saddle rings hang bags of soy beans, and a satchel on the saddle horn, a bag of dried rice on the rear saddle horn and horse shoes on the rear saddle rings, so that they are fixed firmly. Always keep hold of the leash tightly and secure the horse to something. Attach the *Kobanagawa* nose-band onto the *Tachigiki* cheek piece to hold him in place and when you feed the horse, loosen and release the bit. As soon as the feeding has finished, retighten the headstall and bit the horse again.[33]

As is apparent in this account, the warrior horse was also something of a beast of burden, although the bulk of major supplies would be carried in the baggage train.

Although the grooms were, in theory, purely present in a supporting role to the military action of the samurai, their close relationship to their master would often take them into the heart of battlefield action. 'Toroku' states that 'there is not such a great chance of being killed', and implies that such a situation might only occur if the enemy were overwhelming the allied forces, and attacking into the rear areas. This being said, Toroku states that if it does look likely that the grooms will be killed, they should try to take at least one of two of the enemy with them.

▲ *Japanese horse armour was usually concentrated around the chest and the head, areas most exposed to missiles during the charge. (Nik Wheeler/Alamy)*

SADDLE TERMINOLOGY

Shizuwa – the cantle (rear lower back support)

Iso – a rear raised mound

Kirigumi – the joint that connects the saddle seat with the saddle board

Tsumasaki – the lower edges of the front and rear saddle board

Suhama/waniguchi – the shape of the saddle boards at the top of the inner curve

Kuradoshi – a slot for holding the stirrup leathers

Tegata – hand grips cut into the saddle boards

Maewa – the front saddle board

Umi – the upper part of the saddle board

Yama – the 'mountain' (the highest point on the saddle boards)

Orime – the mound ridge

Igiai – the saddle seat

LOGISTICS

Except for the most localised campaigns, when supplies could be light, the samurai army on the march had to transport a heavy burden of food and equipment over long distances, all while clad in armour and shod in simple straw sandals. There were two essential ways in which this load was carried: personally by the warriors and their retainers, and on the baggage train.

▲ *The Japanese Kiso breed of horse, still in existence today, is stocky and strong, an ideal animal for handling campaign logistics and rough living. (Eiko/CC-BY-SA-2.0)*

PERSONAL LOAD-CARRYING

The wealthiest of samurai would have an assortment of servants and retainers to help carry their loads. The *Zōhyō Monogatari* lists numerous such individuals, whose menial roles nevertheless carried with them a large amount of responsibility. The *mochiyari katsugi* (spear-carrying servant) 'Kichinaizaemon', for example, recounts an incident in which while he was asleep, a silver binding clamp was stolen from his master's spear, a crime for which Kichinaizaemon feared he would be blamed and executed. In very dramatic fashion, he goes on to tell how he attempted to tip the balance of favour in his direction by demonstrating battlefield bravery. Launching himself into action with a spear, he was nearly killed, but eventually managed to bring an enemy warrior off his horse, then followed up by cutting off the samurai's head with a *wakizashi*. Retrieving the enemy's head, sword and spear put Kichinaizaemon beyond reproach for the loss of the silver clamp, although he reflected somewhat anxiously that such a small thing as a clasp nearly cost him his life.

Hasamibako mochi (box-carrying servants) transported the master's equipment and personal effects in either a wooden or a wicker box, the latter being much preferred because of its lightness when compared to solid wood. The *yabako mochi* (arrow-carrying servant) would be responsible for direct arrow supply to bowmen. The arrows themselves were stored

◀ *A kabuto (helmet), featuring nami-gata tate hagi-no ita (wave shaped helmet plates). (Samuraiantiqueworld/CC-BY-SA-3.0)*

▼ *Japanese forces gather themselves just prior to the Battle of Akasaka (1274), which inflicted another defeat on the invading Mongols. (CC-PD)*

in large wooden boxes of 100–200 arrows, and ideally they were carried on packhorses, but during a campaign it was not uncommon for them to be carried by the *yabako mochi* themselves. The *yabako mochi* in the *Zōhyō Monogatari*, 'Yazo', explains that carrying the arrow boxes on the shoulder was both awkward and painful; strapping the box to the back like a backpack was far more convenient and comfortable. He also recounts watching arrow carriers from other units struggling to carry the heavy boxes over mountainous terrain, each box handled by two people, one at each end. At one point, two men dropped the box, the lid broke open and the arrows scattered around the terrain, many of them being trodden on and broken by other troops. The *yabako mochi* were not just men of burden, however. They were also responsible for checking the condition of the arrows, ensuring that shafts were unsplit, bindings tight, fletchings unbroken and arrow heads securely in place.

The *tamabako mochi* (bullet-box-carrying servant) was the firearms equivalent of the *yabako mochi*. The bullet boxes themselves were heavy items, and were therefore either carried on a packhorse or suspended from a pole and carried on the shoulders of two men.

In addition to the 'carrying' servants, a samurai army would have also been accompanied by significant numbers of *bumaru* (labourers), whose job it would be to perform any manual tasks required to support operations, such as building camp fences, collecting firewood and erecting any siege works.

All of the individuals just mentioned above were not samurai, but members of the peasantry and labouring classes. This does not appear to mean that they were entirely without status. The author of the *Zōhyō Monogatari* seem keen to imbue their characters not only with a sense of pride in their service, but he also points to how several of the servants have their own armour and weapons, and hence might be expected to contribute to the fight.

We must not get the impression that the samurai warrior himself was happily free of clutter and burden, with servants to carry all his equipment and effects. In fact, most samurai would load themselves heavily with equipment, either through a lack of servants or to ensure that they were ready to fight immediately, should the need arise. Much like the modern US Marine Corps soldier, a samurai in-theatre was not expected to go anywhere without the means to fight and defend himself. Personal responsibility for equipment was also imposed by Japanese terrain, as the mountainous terrain limited the possibilities for using wagons and carts – vehicles that formed the bedrock of European logistics.

Thus, the samurai would go on the march in full armour and carrying his personal weapons. The armour alone must have made the experience of campaigning a taxing one. In summertime, he would sweat profusely inside his metal and fabric wrappings, with a real risk of heat exhaustion. Although the lacquered plates themselves were impressively resistant to corrosion, the bindings that attached them together would have been degraded by the sweat and the sunlight, and in winter by the rain and snow. For this reason, an essential part

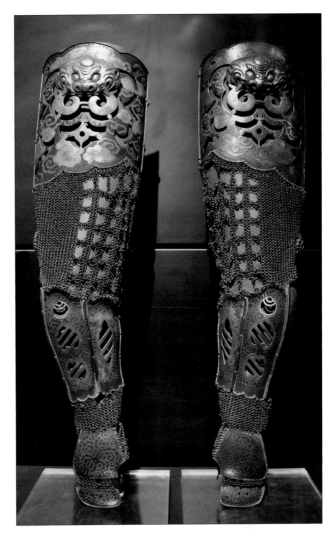

▲ *Highly ornate Edo period samurai armour sleeves, signed by Myochin Ki no Munesada, and made in iron and silver. (Vasil/CC-Zero)*

▼ *Edo period* sode *shoulder armour. On campaign, the lacing could become home to many parasites, and would need to be cleaned or replaced. (Samuraiantiqueworld/C-BY-SA-3.0)*

▲ *The site of Mōri Hidemoto's position in the Battle of Sekigahara located in Tarui, Gifu. Mōri was a senior Toyotomi retainer and commander. (CC-BY-SA-3.0)*

of the samurai's personal kit was some basic armour repair tools and a length of strong cord. Other equipment to aid field life included a personal grooming kit, especially for shaving, cleaning the nails and preparing his hair every morning, as well as writing implements, spare sandals etc. He would also have the accoutrements for fire starting and signalling, including torch materials, flammable oils, flint and striker, an ember-carrying cylinder and possibly an iron fire basket.

The rest of the samurai's personal equipment depended much on the weapon that he carried. If he had an arquebus, for example, he would have a box of *hayago* cartridges hanging from his waist sash, plus a container of musket balls, a flask of spare powder and extra lengths of match. If an archer, he would wear a quiver of arrows on his right hip. Stephen Turnbull also points out that the lancers did not get off lightly because of their simple weapon; they might actually be required to carry boxes of gunpowder, cartridges and arrows, or even signalling drums and kitchen equipment.[34] Everyone had to play his part in transporting the army to war.

BAGGAGE TRAIN

For extensive campaigns, the samurai army would have been supported by a dedicated baggage train, consisting largely of a heavily laden mass of packhorses and human carriers. The baggage train was essential if the campaign was to extend for more than four or five days, the length of time the warriors could fend for themselves on personal stocks of food (see overleaf).

The commander of the logistics and baggage train was the

◄ *Although this procession in 2011 numbered just 82 men, it still gives a good idea of the spectacle of a Japanese army on the march. (LE PICTORIUM/Alamy)*

konida bugyo. It could be an awkward position to fill, as it offered little in the way of martial glamour, but its significance to the overall success of a campaign was paramount. The enemy was also fully aware of the importance of the baggage train, and would try to capture or destroy it if the opportunity presented itself, thus the *konida bugyo* had to be as much of the warrior mindset as that of the logistician. For this reason, the role was occupied by a person of high status and impeccable credentials.

This being said, the *konida bugyo* was typically only required if the baggage train was formed as a single mass entity (*bette no konida oshi*), the horses and men placed at the rear of the marching column. An alternative approach was to have smaller individual baggage sections attached to the specific units of the army, each headed by a quartermaster.

The *Scroll of Earth* from the Natori-ryu provides a detailed insight into some of the considerations and practicalities of managing a baggage train. A particularly interesting point regards the ratios of personnel to horses. The writer states that if the baggage train has a total complement of 100 packhorses, then the commander should assign a total of 1,000 men (typically *ashigaru* foot soldiers or armed servants) purely for the defence of the baggage train, in addition to the c. 1,000 managing the animals and goods. Although many packhorses would carry only the supplies, with the humans walking alongside them, some horses (*noriake*) would be mounted, but if the baggage train had to defend itself the riders were instructed to dismount to participate in the defence.

It is obvious from this division of labour that security concerns were uppermost in the commander's mind. Security was not just a matter of protecting against enemy forays, although they were the most serious threat, but also against internal pilfering and petty theft. If a unit was running low on food or ammunition, a well-stocked baggage train attached to another unit must have been a tempting prospect. To ensure that supplies were properly allocated, supply boxes were typically designated with unit markings.

The packhorses would not just carry food, weaponry and armour, but also a selection of tools to perform the essential duties of camp life and campaign engineering. The Natori-ryu describe the contents of the *konida tsuzura no koto*, cylindrical wicker baskets with semicircular lids, carried on the horses' flanks. The tools stored within each basket are listed as:

- ◼ hammer
- ◼ sickle
- ◼ saw
- ◼ drill
- ◼ hatchet
- ◼ nails
- ◼ cutters
- ◼ hook and rope
- ◼ hoe with rounded edge
- ◼ hoe with square edge
- ◼ rake
- ◼ thin rope

▲ *With ranks of* ashigaru *following up behind, the great Oda Nobunaga moves his campaigning army past clearly intimidated villagers.* (Ukiyo-e/CC-PD-Mark)

▼ *A fine example of a Japanese* sashimono, *which would be worn on the back of a samurai as a unit identifier.* (Samuraiantiqueworld/CC-BY-SA-3.0)

FOOD AND RATIONS

Maintaining adequate food supplies was a priority consideration, especially in the winter months or during long siege actions. Because of the mountainous nature of Japan, the opportunities for foraging and authorised pillaging could be scant, depending on the density of population in the campaign region.

Apart from rice, Japan has little in the way of major mass agriculture, so unlike in many European campaigns, the Japanese commander could make no assumptions about living off the land. Furthermore, during times of war, the local people themselves might be starving. The Natori-ryu gave guidance to the baggage train commander to be vigilant for attacks by local village people, intent on stealing the goods.

Each warrior, samurai and *ashigaru* alike, carried only his personal supply of rice, sufficient to last about four to five days. The rice was prepared in individual portions of raw rice or cooked riceballs (*onigiri*), each portion being tied in a section of a long sack, up to 15 individual portions in length. These rice portions, along with perhaps some dried and salted fish and vegetables, formed the basis of the samurai's field rations, with anything beyond that requirement being kept on the baggage train.

If pillaging was authorised, foraging parties would go out in search of food. This activity was complicated by the fact that many local people, knowing that a hungry army was on its way, would often hide their food in advance. Quartermasters gave instructions to foraging parties to search pots and kettles inside the houses, where food might be stored. More industrious hiding involved burying wrapped quantities of food in the ground outside; foragers were told to scan the ground visually on frosty mornings, as the place of burial was often revealed by a different texture of frost covering the disturbed ground, in contrast to the ground around it.

The landscape was also scoured for its natural larder, especially seeds, nuts and roots, which provided a high degree of nutrition and energy. When times were particularly hard, some ingenuity could fill the gap. For example, in the *Zōhyō Monogatari* the quartermaster cautions his subordinates not to

◀ *Using a cattle-pulled carriage, Emperor Nijō (r. 1158–65) escapes from the Imperial Palace to the Rokuhara mansion. (Tokyo Digital Museum/ CC-PD-Mark)*

◀ *Priests make an incense offering for Oda Nobunaga at Daitoku-ji Temple in Kyoto. Many rites were performed before battle was joined. (Yoshitoshi/ CC-PD-Mark)*

throw away pack ropes or the straw lids from rice containers. As he explains, the ropes are often made from edible plant fibres, especially taro, so cutting them into sections and boiling them could result in a tasteless but consumable soup. The straw lids for the baskets could be similarly prepared, although not for human eating – rather, they provided forage for horses.

Field cooking was naturally over an open fire, or within improvised earthen ovens. Cooking equipment carried with the army included a variety of kettles, pots, bamboo steamers and, more ingeniously, the *irekonabe no koto*, or fitted pan set. This was a set of copper or iron pans, of decreasing dimensions, stacked inside one another and stored in a wooden box. The pan set was an excellent space-saving measure. A cooking pot with almost comic practicality was the *chodo*, which was made again of copper or iron, but was shaped like a helmet so that it could be worn *as* a helmet by a servant in battle. The *chodo* also evidently had some musical resonance, as it could be beaten with a wooden spoon as a signalling device.

Clean drinking water, for both horses and men, was another campaign challenge. In enemy territory, it was common for the army's opponents to poison wells and any body of standing water with faeces or the corpses of dead animals, spreading disease among all those who drank the water. For this reason, it was recommended that the warriors only drink from fast-flowing rivers and streams. The *Zōhyō Monogatari* does give some slightly misguided advice about purifying water. One tip is to take apricot stones and boil them in the water, the stones making the water safe to drink, although in reality the boiling achieved that. Another method was to dry out snails taken from rice fields back home, and then boil these in water to render it potable.

The campaigning samurai army must have been an impressive sight to behold: ornate, dynamic and threatening. The true test of the quality of this army, however, would only come on the actual battlefield, the subject of our next chapter.

CAMPS

The samurai armies were not big camp builders, largely due to the challenges of transporting tents and other structural materials on the campaign. While the most senior commanders of the army would generally commandeer temples and houses, the rest of the army would sleep wherever opportunity presented itself, including farm buildings and caves. The samurai were also adept at what we might today term 'survival camping', making improvised beds from platforms of tree boughs (especially fir) to insulate them from the ground, and using trees, bushes and wooden branches to give a measure of overhead protection.

A military camp would also include a *honjin* command centre, essentially a space marked out for the military leaders using large curtains. If the camp was to be occupied for some days, however, the labourers typically got to work constructing fences of various forms, these being used both to provide a measure of perimeter security and also to corral horses into a controllable space. The Natori-ryu gave quite detailed instructions for the types of fence that could be built, ranging from simple posts connected by rope through to diamond-shaped bamboo lattices. There is also guidance on how to set up pitfall traps, locating these in places that the enemy might use to approach the army's position, such as narrow paths or steep sections of ground. The pitfall trap would consist of a hinged trap door in the ground, disguised with soil and plants, with caltrops or spikes at the bottom to injure the enemy men or horses should they be unlucky enough to fall through.

▼ *Examples of samurai* uma-jirushi *battle standards, which were large, three-dimensional, and came in all manner of designs. (Harold B. Lee Library/CC-PD)*

▼ *Musicians would be part of many aspects of campaign life, from providing courtly entertainment (as seen here) to delivering battlefield commands. (Peter Horree/Alamy)*

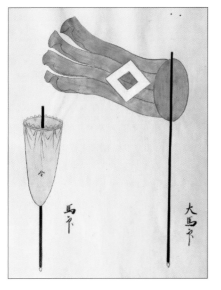

田信玄旗 白地效黒箱之□

武田代之旗也

諏訪法性上下大明神

白地耳青文字赤

十三

CHAPTER SEVEN

THE SAMURAI IN BATTLE

COMMAND, CONTROL AND COMBAT

In this chapter, we will attempt to distil the fundamental principles of samurai war making, mainly as it was during the Sengoku *jidai*. By and during this era, profound changes had come across Japanese warfare. Army sizes had grown exponentially, principally through the addition of the *ashigaru* troops that actually came to constitute the bulk of a *daimyō*'s army. With growth came both an increase in the scale of battles – engagements with more than 50,000 men on the battlefield were witnessed – and the need to manoeuvre the mass formations in a tactically ordered and meaningful way. Thus, the days of emboldened samurai launching their unilateral charges to prove their valour were, by the 15th century, largely gone. In fact, the writings of the Natori-ryu threatened punishments for samurai who made tactical decisions that hadn't been issued or authorised by the higher command. The samurai armies of the Sengoku period were to all intents and purposes mixed-arms formations that needed rigorous control if they were to be battle-winning.

◄ *Various war banners, each proclaiming the identity of the bearer and the unit around him. The banner on the left, for example, is that of the Taira clan, the words translating as 'God of 98,000 armies'. (Seiki Shuzu/CC-PD)*

STRUCTURE AND FORMATIONS

Compared to modern armies, the command structures of samurai armours can appear of Byzantine complexity. Within the samurai themselves this is especially true, as command and seniority emerged from a complex mix of factors, including wealth, ancestry, family name, clan traditions and so on, with variations from region to region and family to family.

The command structure among the *ashigaru* is somewhat more accessible, given its division into specified units of size and weapon type, led by fixed-title commanders. We shall take a top-down view by looking at those principal figures who guided battlefield decision-making, big and small. As always, however, we should be mindful of the permutations and differences.

THE MAKU

Before explaining individuals, further notes are required about the *maku*, which was in effect a portable field command centre. As introduced in the previous chapter, the *maku* consisted of heavy fabric curtains, ropes and iron poles, dismantled and carried while on the march but assembled on a patch of defensible ground set as the headquarters (*honjin*). The *maku* would be visible to surrounding troops through means of various flags and standards (see page 138). Inside the *maku*, despite the seniority of the inhabitants, the

furnishing was very plain, scarcely more than stools and a table. As the *maku* had little in the way of physical security – occasionally a temporary palisade might be created outside – protection for the occupants was provided by the *hatamoto*, essentially the *daimyō*'s personal bodyguard and household entourage, as well as the wider formations, who were mindful of the need to protect their leader at all costs.

HIGH COMMAND AND SAMURAI COMMANDERS

The high command of every samurai army was highly variable. The *daimyō*'s governmental and military structure was defined by his *kashindan*, a collective term for the totality of his family and social relations that together formed his power base. Beneath the *daimyō* would be a collection of individuals occupying positions of authority and influence. An insight into how this upper echelon of the command structure might appear is found on the *Heieki Yoho* scrolls of the

◀ *Sat beneath his standard, here we see the samurai warrior and general Sengoku Hidehisa (1552–1614), who rose to become the head of the Komoro Domain in Shinano Province. (CC-PD-Mark)*

▼ *Part of the* Mōko Shūrai Ekotoba, *a set of two Japanese illustrated handscrolls composed between 1275 and 1293 to show scenes from the Mongol invasion of Japan. (CC-PD-Mark)*

Natori-ryu, in a section entitled 'An Outline of High-Ranking Military Positions'. At the top of the hierarchical tree was the *jo-shōgun*, or supreme leader of a particular force. In samurai terminology, we often find that certain terms are interchangeable with others, creating some confusion for historians and probably contemporaries alike. Hence, we also see the supreme military leader given the title *dai-shōgun*. This latter title appears in a very useful list in the *Heieki Yoho*, in which it defines both the senior positions in an army and also how those positions related to a specific army structure. Referring to the *Gunboryo* document, a chapter from an 8th-century military work, the writer lists the highest levels of command as the following:

- *dai-shōgun* (supreme military commander)
- *fuku-shōgun* (deputy shogun)
- *gungen* (military supervisors)
- *gunso* (senior military officers)

Two positions missing from this list (but acknowledged in the *Heieki Yoho*) are the *sa-shōgun* (Shogun of the Left) and the *u-shōgun* (Shogun of the Right). Both of these are in effect senior generals, to be inserted between the *dai-shōgun* and the *fuku-shōgun*. The roles of these are clarified in that when an entire army is divided into three divisions, the *dai-shōgun*, *sa-shōgun* and *u-shōgun* each have command of a division. Two other shogun ranks given are the *chu-shōgun* (middle shogun) and *ka-shōgun* (lower shogun), the middle shogun stepping in as the *fuku-shōgun* and the *ka-shōgun* as the *chu-shōgun,* should battlefield developments demand permanent or temporary replacement of senior figures.

▲ *Sasaki Moritsuna leads his men and horses across the narrow strait between Kojima and Honshū during the Battle of Fujito (1184). (Utagawa Kuniyoshi/CC-PD-Mark)*

Clarifying the high-command structure further, the Natori-ryu explains that an army of 10,000 men will have (in descending order of seniority): one *shōgun*, one *fuku-shō gun*, two *gungen*, four *gunso* and four *rokuji* (military secretaries). The numbers are obviously adjusted depending on the size of the force. For an entire *sangun* – essentially three armies combined into the entire force sent by the *daimyō* – the command consisted of one *dai-shōgun*, three *shōgun*, four *fuku-shōgun*, ten *gunso* and eight *rokuji*.[35] At the smaller levels of unit command, the Natori-ryu recommended that for a troop of 100–150 soldiers, a single *samurai-daisho* (samurai commander) is required, although the author recognised that some clans might assign two such men to this position.

One particularly important frontline commander of battlefield samurai units was the *ikusa-bugyo*, or 'minister of war'. As the Natori-ryu clarifies:

The *ikusa-bugyo* control everything within an army. They consider everything in discussion with the *hata-bugyo* flag commanders and the *yari-bugyo* spear commanders. Their task is to give orders concerning combat. During battle, they move around to see each unit, so they are also described as *uki-masha* – floating warriors. They ensure that the formations are correctly constructed, check the samurai troops and give them direct orders, discussing any concerns with each unit. Particularly in an army of the small number, they sometimes take command of the unit wherever it is deemed to be necessary, although this varies from clan to clan.[36]

SAMURAI UNITS

While the above is a very useful and precise guide to the samurai high command, the composition of the upper echelons of an army was very much subject to the decisions of the *daimyō* and the traditions of his clan. A specific insight into contextual samurai command structure comes from the *Kōyō Gunkan* of the Takeda family, mentioned in the previous chapter. The army campaigning in 1573 was split into three main parts: the *jikishindan*, the *sakikata-shu* and the *kuni-shu*. The *jikishindan* was the inner circle of the *daimyō*, and broke down into four sections:

▶ *An ancient set of Japanese armour. Note the armour plate over the centre chest, covered with embossed leather. (Rama/CeCILL)*

▼ *A re-enactor's samurai armour. This view shows how much the* shikoro *of the* kabuto *protected the back of the neck. (Prisma by Dukas Presseagentur GmbH/Alamy)*

1. *goshinrui-shu* – the immediate family members of the *daimyō*
2. *go fudai karo-shu* – these were the *daimyō*'s chief retainers and his hereditary vassals
3. *ashigaru-taisho* – the generals in command of *ashigaru*
4. *hatamoto shoyakunin* – the lord's guards and personal attendants, a large composite group including samurai, *ashigaru* and servants

One point to note about these groupings was that they did not just supply leaders, they were also significant elements of the military force. The *goshinrui-shu* and *go fudai karo-shu*, for example, were large repositories of samurai mounted troops.

Beyond the *jikishindan*, the *sakikata-shu* consisted of enemies who had previously been defeated in battle, but had subsequently defected to service with the rival *daimyō*. The

NINJA

Like the samurai, the ninja are another legendary warrior group in Japanese history, although far less is known about their actual activities than the samurai. The role and talents of the ninja, furthermore, have been excessively embellished by modernity, which presents them as somewhere between special forces and superheroes. In reality, the *shinobi no mono* (men of secrecy) – the term ninja was far less common – were essentially men skilled in what we might today call 'covert operations': espionage, secret intelligence gathering, sabotage, infiltration (often using stealth, subterfuge or disguise) and occasionally assassination. Outright physical combat was not typically a goal of *shinobi*; indeed, if a ninja found himself in a fight, then it was likely that his mission had gone awry. Intead individual ninja warriors were used for missions such as infiltrating castles under siege, spying on enemy commanders or forces, or planting disinformation among the enemy. Occasionally, they might be required to assassinate an enemy VIP, as discreetly as possible. Ninja origins are unclear, certainly ancient, but their period of peak influence was the 12th–16th centuries; once Japan was stabilised under the Tokugawa shogunate, many ninja became effectively redundant. During their heyday, however, they were mostly mercenary in nature, hired by warlords who needed their particular talents to gain an advantage in a political or military campaign.

▲ *A samurai* kabuto *(helmet) with a crest fashioned in the shape of a crouching rabbit. (Metropolitan Museum of Art/ Rogers Fund, 1907/Marie-Lan Nguyen/CC-BY-SA-2.5)*

THE HATAMOTO

Those who belonged to the *hatamoto* were a true samurai elite, men who had been picked for the closest of service to their lord. They formed a ferociously loyal bodyguard element to the *daimyō*, in the form of both mounted and foot soldiers, but certain members of the *hatamoto* would also assist the *daimyō* in managing and commanding his army, including providing tactical and strategic guidance. Their bond to the *daimyō*, however, was not familial bloodlines, but a direct oath of fealty.

At the summit of the *hatamoto* hierarchy was the *karo*, an individual (or individuals – some *daimyō* appointed more than one) who operated in a very close personal relationship with the lord, even to the extent of acting as trusted deputies on campaign or in the *daimyō*'s absence from his fortress.

A larger group of influential *hatamoto*s were known as the *bugyo* (commissioners), who actually had practical military command obligations not just over frontline troops, but also for support functions such as logistics. As Stephen Turnbull clarifies, the *bugyo* 'were the general staff officers within a *daimyō*'s army who provided, among other services, strategic and tactical advice.'[37] Adjectives clarify the exact command responsibilities of the *bugyo*. The *yari bugyo*, for example, was in charge of everything relating to the acquisition, distribution, quality and use of spear weapons, both among the samurai and the *ashigaru*. Other positions included the *teppo bugyo* (firearms and archery commissioner), *shodogu bugyo* (equipment commissioner) and *fune bugyo* (boat commissioner), among many other possibilities. Another category of influential official within the *hatamoto* was the *yokome* (inspectors), who were effectively in charge of monitoring and recording discipline, both on and off the battlefield.

The mounted and foot soldiers within the *hatamoto* were warriors of some status within the *daimyō*'s army, typically samurai of high personal standing within the military and wider society. Some of the guardsmen would possess significant individual wealth, and thus brought with them their own minor force of attendants and soldiers.

▲ *A battle screen depicting a clash in the Hōgen rebellion, 1156. The conflict lasted less than a month, and was fought to decide an issue of imperial succession. (CC-PD-Mark)*

kuni-shu, which can be translated as 'provincial corps', were essentially a form of part-time militia, a mixture of social elements either unemployed or partly employed put to temporary military service.

As we can see here, the sources of influence that fed into military command structures during this period were extremely complex. As with modern armies, there was a hierarchy, but a hierarchy that contained within it elements of meritocracy, tradition, seniority and sheer power.

ASHIGARU COMMANDERS

The command structure for the *ashigaru* is a little more accessible than that for the samurai. As has been noted previously, the *ashigaru* were subdivided into several subcategories, based primarily on either their weapons or their functions – arquebusier, archer, spearman, attendant, musician etc. The overarching command of the *ashigaru* army lay with the *ashigaru-taisho*, a person of samurai rank and considerable standing within the army as a whole.

The next step down in the *ashigaru* rank system was the *ashigaru kashira*, in effect a sort of company commander, although the size of the company could be significantly smaller than we understand it today, sometimes just a few dozen men, but might also be as high as about 200. Finally, the smallest unit of men (the *buntai*) were led by the *ashigaru kogashira*, each of these relatively junior officers leading a group of about 30 men. The *ashigaru kogashira* would have weapon specialisms, such as the *teppo ashigaru kogashira* in charge of musket units.

FORMATIONS

The Japanese armies of the Sengoku *jidai* were mixed-arms formations. The core tactical unit was the *zonae*, which consisted of anywhere between 300 and 800 men, and within

THE EIGHT KEY JAPANESE FORMATIONS

Taking the aggregate of the formations from the Natori-ryu, plus those from other sources, we can establish the eight key formations as the following:

Hoshi **(arrowhead)** – As the name evokes, the *hoshi* formation was aggressive and offensive. Arquebusiers led the way, with seven ranks arranged in echelon to form an arrowhead shape. This shape was then mirrored in the organisation of samurai units behind, and the samurai arrowhead was supported by *ashigaru* troops both to the flanks and the rear. The overall arrowhead profile of the formation meant that it was best used to strike at weak points in the enemy structure, the widening shape of the arrowhead providing a degree of flank protection as well as the capacity to develop an ever-increasing breach in the enemy lines.

Wangetsu **(the crescent moon)** – In this formation, the front ranks consisted of linear formations of arquebusiers, archers and spearmen (listed in order of their presentation), behind which were the samurai troops arranged in asymmetric quarter circles around and behind the HQ, with three lines of arquebusiers and archers forming the rearguard. This formation was primarily defensive, the ranks of the infantry providing a deep defence to the front and rear, while the samurai troops could form up quickly to react to flanking threats.

Kakuyoku **(the crane's wing)** – Nearly half of the depth of this formation (the front half) is composed of multiple ranks of arquebusiers, archers and spearmen, the archers sandwiched between the other weapon types. This powerful body of troops would hit the enemy hard with missile weapons and spear strikes, softening them up for exploitation by the samurai behind. The reference to the 'crane's wing' comes from the arched structure of the first samurai company behind the foot soldiers, with other companies further behind in various concave and convex lines. The samurai were well positioned both to make frontal attacks but also to move out and then in to develop forward envelopments of the weakened enemy units. The *kakuyoku* was also a good defensive formation for resisting a *hoshi* attack.

Gyorin **(fish scales)** – The *gyorin* was similar to a rounded *hoshi*, with the samurai arranged in a convex forward company (plus ranks of *ashigaru* in front) with convex second company units radiating out from the flanks. This formation was recommended for an army that was numerically inferior to its enemy, as it offered a constant offensive forward pressure (and hence was very much in keeping with the samurai spirit) but it spread the forces, and to a certain extent the risk, when contrasted with the more 'all-or-nothing' *hoshi*.

Choda **(long snake)** – Bearing in mind the comment above about Japanese formations leaning towards length rather than width, the *choda* was actually a relatively long and thin formation, with good flank protection plus a vanguard of troops held in the middle to turn defence into attack at the opportune moment. This formation was useful when threatened by the enveloping movements of a *kakuyoku*.

Hoen/saku **(keyhole)** – This ornate formation featured a central circle of samurai, providing a full 360-degree defence. At the 11 o'clock and 1 o'clock positions on the circle, ranks of arquebusiers and archers branched out forwards at a 45-degree angle, thus forming a 'V' shape into which (all going to plan) the enemy advanced and found themselves caught in a crossfire between the missile troops. At the base of the 'V', at the 12 o'clock position in front of the samurai circle, a rank of waiting spearmen provided a further impediment to enemy advance forwards. To the rear of the main samurai circle, linear blocks of samurai troops acted as deep flank defence, and a smaller protective circle surrounded the commander's battle HQ. The *saku* was regarded as an especially practical defence against a *hoshi*.

Ganko **(flying geese)** – *Ganko* is the most linear of the classic eight battle formations. It consists of multiple parallel but offset units, starting with the arquebusiers, then the archers, followed by the samurai and finishing up to the rear with more arquebusiers and archers. There were also smaller units of arquebusiers and archers on the flanks. The heavy concentrations of missile troops meant that fire could be quickly redirected to face emerging threats from almost any direction. The extensive depth of the formation also meant that it could 'soak up' the moment of a heavy enemy charge, progressively taking the impetus out of the enemy troops as they battled through multiple lines.

Koyaku **(yoke)** – So called from its admittedly loose resemblance to the yoke worn by an oxen, *koyaku* had the usual strong front ranks of foot soldiers, behind which the first rank of samurai were arranged in a convex shape, rather like the profile of a shallow food bowl. The samurai companies behind were linear blocks, either facing forwards or out to the flanks. This formation was regarded as a good general defence, especially while trying to ascertain the enemy's intentions and then launch a counter-strike.

whose ranks were contained all types of troops within the army: *ashigaru* and samurai, mounted and unmounted, firearms, spears and bows. When multiple *zonae* were combined together they formed a *te*, while the individual weapon-based sub-units within each *zonae* were called *kumi* or *gumi*.

The Natori-ryu scrolls also make some interesting clarifications about the general organising structure of an army in the field. It outlines what is defined as the 'Seven-Layered Formation':

1. *ichi no saki* – the first troop/vanguard
2. *ni no saki* – the second troop
3. *wakizonae* – flanking troops
4. *hatamoto* – command group
5. *ushirozonae* – rear troop
6. *konida* – logistics and baggage train
7. *yugun* – reserve troop

The author also explains that an eighth layer of soldiers, the *shingari* or 'rear-protecting troops', could be added if the army was to effect a fighting retreat.

The commanders on the Japanese battlefield had to arrange these elements intelligently, the formations best reflecting their offensive or defensive choices. In this matter, the commanders were assisted somewhat by a vast body of traditional battle formations, the absorption of which would have been an intrinsic part of their martial education.

There were literally dozens of recommended formations passed down through history, each with its own peculiar descriptive title, such as *gyorin* (fish scales), *choda* (long snake), *garyo* (reclining dragon) and *shogi-gashira* (captain of chess). The roots of many of the formations went back into ancient Chinese military theory, albeit adapted in the Sengoku period for the new types of weaponry and the emerging styles of warfare. Some of these formations were accessibly simple and could be adopted quickly without excessive manoeuvring. A good example is the *Nanasonae* (Seven Units), which was constructed from three units in the vanguard, two protecting the flanks, the *daimyō* and his retinue/bodyguard in the centre rear, and a rearguard force. Note that regardless of the formation chosen, it was common for

▼ *Ashigaru headgear was typically the* nerigawa toppai jingasa*, a conical war hat made of cheap and durable rawhide. (Samuraiantiqueworld/CC-BY-SA-3.0)*

the *daimyō* to be located centre rear, this position providing him with the greatest levels of protection from enemy incursions. Another noticeable element of many Japanese battle formations, in contrast to much of European warfare, was that formations tended to be deeper than they were wide. Much of the reason for this comes from the very nature of Japanese terrain, which rarely presented the armies with wide, unobstructed battlefields. When the manoeuvre was through broken, steep and complex terrain, thinner formations were better than wider ones.

Although, as noted, there was a long list of battle formations to choose from, eight Chinese structures in particular became almost canonical, these known as the *hachijin*. In the Natori-ryu, these were listed in their Chinese names as:

- *ten* (heaven)
- *chi* (earth)
- *kaze* (wind)
- *kumo* (cloud)
- *ryu* (dragon)
- *tora* (tiger)
- *tori* (bird)
- *hebi* (snake)

The eight Chinese formations are then listed by 'Commentator one' in their Japanese versions as:

- *minote* (the crescent blade)
- *hoshi* (the arrowhead)
- *wangetsu* (the crescent moon)
- *ichimonji* (the single line)
- *ganko* (the flying geese)
- *suginari* (arrowhead with horizontal lines)
- *gyorin* (fish scale)
- *kakuyoku* (the crane's wing)

'Commentator two' also lists the Japanese formations, with a slight variation on the first list, replacing *ganko* with *ichigyo* (the single column).[38] Not all of the formations are precisely clear historically, although their descriptive names, which allude to shape, give a decent hint of their tactical principles. For example, there are implicit references to curved ranks of troops, either concave or convex. Convex units (i.e. bulging out towards the enemy) could deflect and blunt attacks, while convex units could fold around an enemy, creating a defence through flanking attack.

Beyond the eight core formations, there were all manner of formations, some being subtle variations on the themes explained in the box, others being complex and now impractical older tactics, and yet others being very much developed for the new age of warfare. The *minotenari* ('winnowing fan'), for example, was a defensive formation with arquebusiers formed up behind bamboo barricades, to

▲ *A samurai warrior in complete battlefield armour, including a half-face* menpō. *Note the presentation of his two blades. (Felice Beato/CC-PD-Mark)*

give them a protective firing position. Two especially important formations, or more specifically movements, were the *kuribuki*, which was essentially a phased withdrawal procedure, and its adaptation called the *kurikomi*, which was used in narrow terrain, the retreating troops moving back in a narrow column but then periodically circling back behind natural features to effect an intermittent defence. Whatever formations the commander chose, they were not set in stone, but had to go through adaptation and improvisation as the battle developed.

CASE STUDY:

FOURTH BATTLE OF KAWANAKAJIMA

The Kawanakajima Plain, Shinano Province (present-day city of Nagano) was a bitterly contested location during the 16th century, with five major battles fought there between 1553 and 1564. Its blight was its location on the border of the territories of Takeda Shingen and Uesugi Kenshin, bitter rivals in the struggle for dominance in central Japan. The plain was ringed with high mountains on all sides, and it was framed by the flow of two rivers – the Saigawa and the Chikumagawa – their meeting in the east of the plain creating a triangular aquatic boundary.

In October 1561, when the fourth battle took place, Takeda Shingen controlled the plain, the most prominent position being his Kaizu Castle, positioned just to the south of the Chikumagawa, although Uesugi controlled much territory to the north of the Saigawa, including the major Buddhist temple of Zenkō-ji. It was the Kaizu that became the focal point of Uesugi's campaign against the Shingen, when in September he advanced out from his base at Kasugayama Castle to the north with some 18,000 troops. Leaving about

▼ *This depiction of a Sengoku period battle perfectly captures the dynamic violence of hand-to-hand fighting, and the tactical centrality of the spear. (CC-PD-Mark)*

3,000 troops at Zenkō-ji, Kenshin marched with the remainder about 70km (43 miles) to the south, crossed the rivers, and positioned his troops on the Saijoyama Mountain overlooking Kaizu Castle. Uesugi's plan was to lure Takeda's main army, centred around the Takeda fortress in Kofu, 130km (80 miles) away, out of its base and into battle at Kawanakajima. Certainly, Kaizu Castle was there for the taking – it was manned by just 150 troops, led by Kosaka Danjo Masanobu. Despite the distance between Kawanakajima and Kofu, Masanobu was able to transmit his situation to Shingen in about two hours, using the established system of signal fires. Responding to the crisis, Shingen mobilised an army of 16,000 men and marched out, with another 4,000 acquired as he passed through Shinano Province. He was accompanied by respected commander and tactician Yamamoto Kansuke, who had served the Takeda since 1543, as an *ashigaru-taisho*. The march from Kofu to Kawanakajima took a total of 24 days. For much of the journey, Shingen kept the Chikumagawa on his right flank, as both security and to shield his intentions as much as possible from the opposing scouts. Finally, he crossed the river and took up positions in and around Kaizu Castle. From Uesugi's perspective, his plan to draw the Takeda into battle was clearly coming to fruition.

By this time, Kansuke had developed a plan to trap Uesugi in a decisive pincer movement. The first part of the plan involved sending 8,000 men, led by Masanobu, on a stealthy night mission to climb Saijoyama Mountain from the rear, then launch a morning attack that would force the Uesugi army down from their elevated position, across the Chikumagawa at the ford of Amenomiya (where the Takeda had also crossed the river during their advance to Kaizu) and on to the Hachiman Plain. Yet, also during the night, Shingen would have led another 8,000 troops furtively down on to the plain, there to establish defensive blocking positions. If all went to plan, the Uesugi army would be trapped between the two Takeda forces and routed.

The problem for Shingen was that Kenshin had got wind of the plan, or had at least acquired intelligence of Takeda movements that enabled him to divine their purpose. So, even as the two Takeda forces began their night-time movements at the stroke of midnight, on 18 October 1561, Kenshin was deploying his army quietly down from the Saijoyama Mountain, aiming to crush the Takeda forces with a surprise attack on its own terms in the early hours of the morning.

As first light began to streak the sky, Shingen and his men were in position on the Hachiman Plain when, to their astonishment, a mass of Uesugi cavalry and foot soldiers surged on to the attack. Both sides had selected their battle formations judiciously. The Takeda had adopted the *kakoyuku*, this formation offering solid defensive characteristics but also the ability to convert quickly into an attack and envelopment.

► *In this close-up of the Siege of Ulsan, samurai mounted archers maintain a steady stream of fire to suppress the defenders on the battlements, while other troops scale the walls with assault ladders. (CC-PD-Mark)*

▼ *This photograph shows a* wakidate tsunamoto, *a bracket used to mount and display the* wakidate *side decoration on the* kabuto. *(Samuraiantiqueworld/CC-BY-SA-3.0)*

Kenshin was to use the *kuruma gakari* ('winding wheel'). The army was formed up in a large circular, turning formation, from which units would be detached to make an assault, then return to the wheel as they tired and lost momentum, their place taken by fresh units. By using this formation, the Uesugi could therefore keep up a relentless pressure on the Takeda frontlines, aiming to maintain this pressure until a collapse was achieved.

The battle was brutal and fast-paced, both sides taking heavy casualties from archery and muskets, and from the spears of the mounted troops and *ashigaru*. Physical fighting occurred even at the highest levels of command. Numerous Uesugi nobles were unseated from their horses and killed or wounded. On the Takeda side, Kansuke, in despair at the evident failure of his tactical master plan, grabbed a spear and charged suicidally into the midst of the enemy, taking dozens of wounds until he felt compelled to commit *seppuku*. At one particularly dramatic point, even Kenshin himself, at the head of his bodyguard, broke into the Takeda *maku*, personally attacking Shingen with his sword while the Takeda lord defended himself with a heavy war fan. A hasty defence by Shingen's retainers and bodyguard troop eventually fought off the close-quarters attack, but it was clear that the battle for Kawanakajima would be a fight for survival across all ranks (Shingen's own brother was killed).

As the morning of battle wore on in increasing bloodshed,

there occurred the event that tipped the clash in favour of the Takeda army. The 8,000 men who had climbed the Saijoyama not only discovered that the enemy there was gone, but also soon heard the sounds of battle from the plain below. Masanobu therefore led his troops at speed back down the mount, heading for the ford of Amenomiya. On reaching the ford, they found their way blocked by a Uesugi guard of 3,000 men, and a desperate action was fought. Yet eventually Masanobu's men achieved a breakthrough, and they rushed across the ford on to the plain. Although Kansuke had by this time already committed suicide, through a circuitous route his plan to achieve a pincer victory was now actually coming to fruition, as the already weakened Uesugi were trapped between two Takeda forces. The winding wheel formation that had served them so well while facing an enemy in a single direction now collapsed under the bi-directional onslaught, and the Uesugi were defeated by midday.

The Takeda had wrested victory from the jaws of defeat, but the price had been high. Exact casualties are difficult to ascertain, but Stephen Turnbull gives figures of 72 per cent casualties for the Uesugi and 62 per cent for the Takeda.[39] The fourth Battle of Kawanakajima illustrates the tactical sophistication that could characterise many large-scale samurai battles, and how the choice of formation was something of a gamble based on predicted outcomes.

BATTLEFIELD COMMAND AND CONTROL

The samurai armies of the Sengoku *jidai* were quite different in many ways from the contemporary armies of Europe, but one problem they all had in common was the issue of command and control once battle was joined.

The main system of command actually took place before the fighting started, and consisted of the training that the units went through prior to engagement, particularly in adopting the chosen combat formation. A well-trained Japanese force could go from a march column to a battle formation in a matter of minutes, as long as the men had been well drilled in the transitions and their respective locations on the battlefield. In addition, any special instructions to leaders were best given prior to the actual clash of arms.

Once battle began, with all its concomitant noise and confusion, the challenge was then to transfer the commander's orders down through the individual units, and

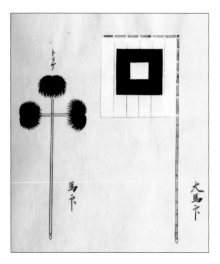

◄ *Large* uma-jirushi *battle standards. These are of Arima Toyouji, a samurai commander who fought in the late 16th and the 17th centuries. (Harold B. Lee Library/ CC-PD)*

▼ *Further scenes from the* Mōko Shūrai Ekotoba. *The scrolls illustrate how important mounted combat was to the samurai in the pre-firearms age. (CC-PD-Mark)*

also for lower-ranking officers to impose some structure upon the behaviour of their men. The overall commander, centrally located in his battle HQ, would give visual indicators of his desire by making understood gestures with his war fan or a war baton. These gestures would be seen by nearby commanders and also by a body of *tsukai-ban* (messengers), extremely important and respected individuals who had the authority to take the leader's will out to the wider world. They would be identifiable by wearing a large *horo* (a basket-like structure that ballooned up with air when the messenger was on the move) on their backs, with a flag on top.

FLAGS AND BANNERS

The chief way in which the Japanese troops oriented themselves on the battlefield was through a bristling network of flags, banners and heraldic symbols. An important example of the latter was the *mon*, effectively a family crest of arms. *Mon* were of highly distinctive designs, with a great variety of floral, figurative, geometric and other types of pattern. The *mon* could appear on many locations: *maku* field curtains; painted on armour, helmets and shields; decorating flags and banners; and displayed on ship's sails. The *mon* provided a useful point of reference for soldiers to check that they were with the units they should be.

Wearing *mon* on individual equipment was no solution to higher-level tactical manoeuvres, and for this purpose there were assorted flags and banners. The location of the *daimyō* or the senior commanding officer would be identifiable by the *o-uma-jirushi* (great standard), a huge flag displaying the emblem of the commander. This flag thereby served as the heart of the army, a place to look towards for leadership and, for the enemy, a focus of their attacks – destroying the HQ

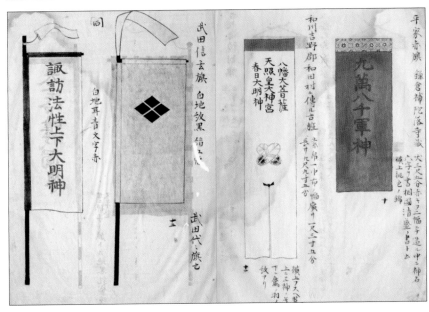

▲ *Four samurai battlefield banners. Allowing banners and heraldry to be captured was seen as a particularly ignominious failure. (Seiki Shuzu/CC-PD)*

▲ *An example of the* sode-jirushi, *essentially a cloth badge worn on the* sode *shoulder plates as a means of personal identification. (Samuraiantiqueworld/CC-BY-SA-3.0)*

and taking the *o-uma-jirushi* would typically be the sign of an army's collapse. As well as the *o-uma-jirushi*, there was the *ko-uma-jirushi* (lesser standard); *daimyō* or commanders of great seniority and military power would carry the pair together, whereas commanders of lower means would only have the *ko-uma-jirushi*. The rules for carrying the two standards were formalised in 1645: those commanders having a wealth of above 1,300 *koku* could bear the *ko-uma-jirushi*, while those of above 6,000 *koku* were also privileged to bear the *o-uma-jirushi* as well.

The two main types of unit banner on the battlefield were the *hata-jirushi* and the *nobori*. Both were banners set in a narrow vertical orientation, the top of the banner suspended from a short horizontal extension from the main shaft. The difference between the two was partly material – the *nobori* were stiffened, whereas the *hata-jirushi* were not – and partly temporal, as the *nobori* emerged during the Sengoku period, largely replacing the *hata-jirushi*.

At an individual level, the *sashimono* worn on the backs of both samurai and some *ashigaru* were the most numerous of the flags. The *sashimono* displayed clan symbols, and often replicated the symbols seen on the larger unit banners. Smaller version of the flags might be worn by the *ashigaru*, although many would just have the *mon* on their armour.[40]

In addition to flags and banners, the samurai armies would also include a large number of more innovative identifying objects, produced from materials such as wood or papier-mâché, often highly coloured, and sculptured into a broad range of designs.

MUSICAL COMMAND

While the Japanese battlefield was crammed with visual orientation, command and control was also achieved through auditory means, specifically drums, conch shells (blown as trumpets) and gongs. As in the traditions of European battlefield instrumentation, each instrument had its own set of rudiments, tunes or patterns that gave specific commands to the surrounding troops. For example, three quick drum beats followed, after a short pause, by five further beats indicated that it was time to make an attack, while four beats–pause– four beats denoted a retreat. An interesting point made by the Natori-ryu was that gongs were mostly used to broadcast retreats, while in the main drums were used for advances. The conch-shell trumpets could emit their commands through tone, pitch, variations in vibrato, length of notes and rhythm.

Taken together, the command-and-control system of the samurai army was actually highly efficient. The striking system of banners and flags meant that it was difficult for a warrior to lose his position except in the most chaotic of battles, while the insistent command music could cut across even the noise of battle. One important consideration, however, was that the enemy knew just how important the banner men and musicians were to the fighting capability of their opponents; the lives of those at the hub of command and control were precarious, and they might be called upon to fight for their own survival.

EXPERIENCE OF BATTLE

Based on the illustrations that have come down to us from history, the experience of combat during the age of the samurai armies was furious, horribly bloody and, at least after the initial exchanges of missile weaponry, fought at close quarters. Some artworks show enraged-looking samurai storming across the battlefield, angrily gripping the severed heads of their victims.

Horses are often depicted crumbling to their knees, shot through with arrows; these unfortunate creatures were as much a target as their riders, and they died in huge numbers from spears, swords, arrows and musket balls. (The *Zōhyō Monogatari* advocates that when faced with a mounted enemy, the arquebusier should always shoot the horse first, then the man.) The ancient battlefields must have been truly soaked in blood.

ARQUEBUSIERS AND ARCHERS

While the violence of war would have been uniform for all, the experience of practical combat at the individual level would have had some variation depending on the type of weapon the soldier wielded, and his personal status. Battles often began, once the armies had closed the distance between them, with heavy exchanges of musket fire and archery, the bows sustaining a rhythm that the rather clumsy arquebuses couldn't match. The musketeers, under the guidance of the *teppo ashigaru kogashira*, would rotate through three ranks of

◄ *The inside view of an Edo period* menpō. *Even with drainage holes, the sweat of battle inside such a mask must have been profound. (Samuraiantiqueworld/CC-BY-SA-3.0)*

SAMURAI MEDICAL CARE

For samurai who suffered serious wounds on the battlefield, the prospects for the future were grim. In an age prior to antibiotics and understanding of infection control, even an initially non-mortal wound could escalate into blood poisoning and ultimate death. The chances of this happening were increased by some of the common medical procedures of the age. For example, applying horse faeces to wounds, even packing it inside the abdominal cavity to treat internal injuries, was an accepted treatment over a period of many centuries, as was the drinking of water mixed with horse faeces to encourage blood clotting. Continuing the theme of the therapeutic properties of horse products, it was also believed that drinking horse blood had coagulant effects.

Any attempt at battlefield surgery was crude at best, life-threatening at worst. The *Zōhyō Monogatari* explains in graphic fashion how arrows stuck in the body should be extracted with chopsticks, the hands or, if the arrow is especially well embedded, with pincers. Should the arrow be stuck in the casualty's face, the recommendation was

to tie his head steady to a tree, then wiggle it free, ignoring the fact that 'while doing this the eye socket will be filled with blood.'

The *Zōhyō Monogatari* contains some further advice for controlling adverse physical conditions on and off the battlefield. For arquebusiers, who would have to cope with the raging thirst induced by the exertion of battle, sunlight and surrounding gunpowder smoke, the top tip was to occasionally take out an umeboshi plum from the ration pack and just look at it, but not eat it or even lick it. If that didn't work, the thirst could be sated by sipping the blood of dead people or drinking the top layer from a muddy pool. On cold days of campaign or battle, it was advised that soldiers rubbed themselves with hot pepper 'from your arse to your tiptoe' to warm themselves up.

Although all manner of traditional medicine might be applied to a severely wounded samurai, the reality of his situation would usually be that he was taken to a quieter part of the battlefield, where he waited for death.

◄ *The female samurai warrior Hangaku Gozen by the artist Yoshitoshi (1839–92). She rose to command thousands of samurai. (Yoshitoshi/CC-PD)*

▲ *This Japanese actor, representing a samurai, illustrates the positioning of the* daishō *sword handles. (Japan Art Collection (JAC)/ Alamy)*

▼ *This scene from the* Mōko Shūrai Ekotoba *shows the brutal reality of battle for horses, this creature clearly dying under repeated arrow strikes. (CC-PD-Mark)*

fire, attempting to maintain a regular rhythm of loading and reloading, despite the evident distractions of battle. The *Zōhyō Monogatari* gives an excellent insight into some of the practicalities of working a musket in battle. The author (adopting the character of a *teppo ashigaru kogashira*) cautions the musketeer to avoid unnecessary rushing, especially when handling cartridges, as this usually results in fumbled loading. He states the clear authority of his position

▲ *The lock mechanism of an antique Japanese matchlock, the hammer (here minus its slowmatch) positioned just over the priming pan. (Samuraiantiqueworld/CC-BY-SA-3.0)*

over the troops: 'While the men in the frontline are shooting, those in the second line should set their *Hinawa* fuses. The target to be aimed at for each distance of 1 *cho* [109m or 119 yards] will be directed by use, that is, those who are in charge.'[41] Notably, the writer also makes it clear that the men will not just fight with their muskets, explaining how when they

▼ *In a scene from the Battle of Yashima (1185), Nasu no Yoichim, mounted on a swimming horse, fires an arrow at the fan on top of the mast of a Taira ship. (CC-PD-Mark)*

get close to the enemy they should draw spears and fight with those, then use swords for true hand-to-hand combat. These descriptions remind us that even the densest and most coordinated of musket fire could not hold back an enemy determined to advance.

The same was true of the bowmen. The *yumi ashigaru kogashira* (bowman sergeant) recommends that even before the fighting commences, the bowmen fix a spearhead or bayonet to the top of their bows, for use when the enemy closes the range. In terms of firing procedure, the sergeant tells the men to take their time and aim properly, and always within the commanded range. He states that one archer should stand between two arquebusiers, only loosing the arrows in the intervals between musket fire, not in synchronicity with it. When the enemy closes to point-blank range, the last arrow should be fired at a spear's-length distance, then the bowman should stab at his enemy's face with the blade affixed to the top of the bow. The author follows with some advice on swordsmanship that could apply to any warrior: 'After that, draw anything you like, such as your sword or your *Wakizashi* short sword, and try to cut the hand or leg of the enemy. Never try to hit the front of the helmet with your weapon; if it is poor in quality, then it will have the edge nicked and it will not function anymore.'[42]

SPEARMEN

The *Zōhyō Monogatari* then turns to the spearmen. The key points for the spearmen are to synchronise the retraction and thrust of their spears as a single unit, overwhelming the enemy defences and maximising the chances of making an

▲ *Kajiwara Kagesue, Sasaki Takatsuna and Hatakeyama Shigetada cross the Uji River before the Second Battle of Uji, 1184. (CC-PD-Mark)*

injurious hit. Indeed, other sources suggest a regimented process of spear-fighting, the spearmen forming ranks of men about 1m (3.3ft) apart and presenting a bristling and uniform barrier, nearly impenetrable to enemy cavalry. The author of the *Zōhyō Monogatari* also points to further applications of the spear, making maximum application of its length. For example, it could be used to strike the shafts of enemy flags and banners, knocking them down and disrupting the opponent's command and control. Regarding the matter of pursuit, however, the writer makes an interesting admonition that the spearmen should not purse a retreating enemy for

more than 1 *cho*. The point was likely that the cavalry were far better suited to pursuit actions than the relatively slow spearmen. Yet, as with nearly all traditional writings about warfare, we have to acknowledge the frequently yawning chasm between theory and practice. Some illustrations, for example, show the spearmen fighting at a running pace in loose order, each man selecting individual targets. Spears would be used to chop, slap and slice the enemy, just as much as they would for making clean piercing blows. The spearmen would also have to master the art of using their spears to deflect incoming blows from enemy spears or

▼ *The great female warrior Tomoe Gozen in battle. The image is interesting partly because it shows the use of the* naginata *from horseback. (CC-PD-Mark)*

SIEGES

Siege warfare was a special and important category within Japanese history, a challenge for both defenders and attackers. For the former, their defence naturally came from the physical structure of the castle (see Chapter 2), the garrison troops, who might number from a few hundred to several thousands, and also the actions they would put into motion when a siege was predicted. At the first signs of an approaching enemy, the defences of the fortress would be checked, repaired and enhanced. In a description of preparations for the siege of Hataya Castle in 1600, the chronicler of the *Oū Eikei Gunki* described how the defenders repaired walls, dug out or deepened defensive ditches, erected palisades, collected supplies of arrows and rice, and took up positions ready for the attack.[43] The chief priorities for the defenders were to ensure that they stored as much food as possible, as some sieges ran to dozens and occasionally hundreds of days. In 1581, for example, Tottori Castle, Inaba Province, was placed under siege by the forces of Oda Nobunaga, the besieging troops under the command of Toyotomi Hideyoshi. Hideyoshi immediately locked a blockade in place, with towers and palisades erected around the perimeter of the fortress.

For good measure, Hideyoshi also purchased virtually all of the rice available in the wider province, to ensure that he controlled the supplies of food. The castle's lord,

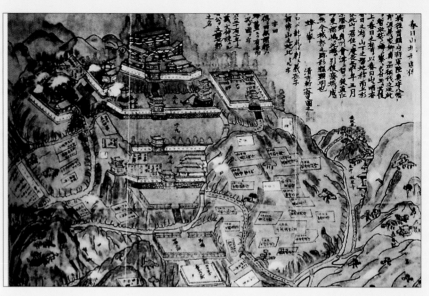

▲ *An old print of Kasugayama Castle, in what is now part of the city of Jōetsu, Niigata Prefecture. The castle was the powerbase of the warlord Uesugi Kenshin. (CC-PD-Mark)*

Kikkawa Tsuneie, had stockpiled as much food as possible for the siege, but was faced with a problem common to all besieged Japanese castles, that of the surrounding peoples, fleeing ahead of the enemy advance, swelling the castle population and stretching food supplies thinner. During the 200-day siege that followed, all animals inside the fortress were eaten, and when the hunger reached terrible extremes there were even instances of cannibalism. The castle was eventually reduced to surrender, Kikkawa Tsuneie committing suicide as part of the surrender deal.

Water supply was also a key factor in the outcome of a

◄ *A night attack on the Sanjō Palace during the Heiji Rebellion in 1160. Fire was the most potent weapon of siege warfare. (Museum of Fire Arts/ CC-PD-Mark)*

▲ *Displayed at the Yasukuni Shrine, a fascinating example of an early breech-loading cannon, from the era of Oda Nobunaga. (Uploadalt/CC-BY-SA-3.0)*

▶ *This* menpō *face mask has an elaborate horsehair moustache. Note also the throat guard* yodare-kake. *(Samuraiantiqueworld/CC-BY-SA-3.0)*

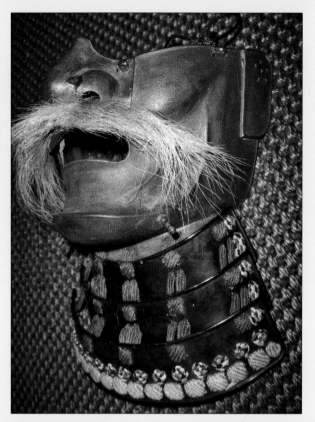

siege. Ideally, the castle would have an internal supply from a spring or inflowing stream, and would collect rainwater through extensive guttering. The enemy, however, would seek to cut off or poison water supplies if possible, an action that could bring a siege to conclusion within a matter of days. Although a castle garrison might make occasional sallies out from the fortress, with the hope of puncturing the enemy siege lines, usually their best hope lay in the arrival of a relief force.

For the besiegers, therefore, it is evident that blockade and starvation were solid options for reducing a fortress, as long as the besiegers themselves could maintain supplies and health during a lengthy investment. For, just as inside the castle, disease could proliferate outside, especially in the form of maladies such as cholera and dysentery.

Of course, a more aggressive option was to make a direct assault, storming the ditches, ramparts, towers and gates of the castle. Supporting fire for the attack came from arquebusiers, archers and cannon, sometimes firing behind large wooden shields for cover. Cannon, however, were somewhat rarer on the Japanese battlefield than on the European one, and they were generally small in calibre or weight of shot, such as a 2lb round shot. There was also a variety of siege engines, at least before cannon came along, including wheeled siege towers, elevated boxes used to hoist archers, arquebusiers or observers up to higher levels, protective wheeled 'tortoise' wagons (for transporting soldiers under cover up to the walls of the fortress), and bundles of bamboo strapped to the front of wheeled carts to act as mobile shields. For scaling walls, infantry might use assault ladders, while undermining by trained labourers could destabilise towers. Yet, whatever means were at their disposal, the besiegers would often find substantial fortresses tough nuts to crack. The defensive fire coming from the castle could be blistering, especially around choke points, and heavy objects would fall like rain from the top of the walls. If several costly attempts did not bring victory, the siege might well be abandoned, but a combination of offensive onslaught and the persistent effects of time would often bring victory.

▼ *The tomb of Minamoto no Yoritomo, today a monument in Kamakura, Kanagawa. (Tarourashima/CC-PD)*

▲ An image of brutal maritime warfare during the 19th-century Satsuma Rebellion. Note how banners are still flown as unit identifiers. (CC-PD-Mark)

▼ The lightweight and foldable (note the hinge at the side) tatami dō tended to be the choice of the less affluent ashigaru. (Samuraiantiqueworld/CC-BY-SA-3.0)

edged weapons, the brief window of time following the deflection presenting the opportunity to strike back.

SAMURAI COMBAT

For the samurai themselves, the techniques of fighting often mirrored those of the *ashigaru* described earlier. Yet although by the 16th century the samurai were not the free-roaming individualists of the past (if indeed they ever really were), but were instead constrained by wider unit considerations, they still expressed their fighting ability through personal combat with, preferably, an identifiable enemy of similar status. The motivation to fight individually came from the system of recording battle events once the fighting had occurred. The greater the exploit, the more personal credit would accrue to the warrior. So, for example, there were battle classifications such as *kumi uchi no komyo*, which meant the act of killing an enemy who was stronger than oneself by using grappling techniques. *Kuzurekiwa no komyo* referred to holding the battle line even as your forces retreated, and *ichiban kubi* denoted the act of taking the first enemy head of the battle. Through these categories, and numerous others like them, the samurai could record his acts, great and small, for posterity. The fight would be brutal and unforgiving. Indeed, as the aforementioned *kumi uchi no komyo* indicates, the act of killing could degenerate to strangulation and outright bare-handed force.

▲ *The fighting at the Honnō-ji Incident (1582), when Oda Nobunaga's retainer Akechi Mitsuhide led a rebellion against him, forcing Oda's suicide. (CC-PD-Mark)*

▼ *The actor Nakamura Shikan, depicting a samurai warrior in battle, prepares to use his bow and arrow. (Science History Images/Alamy)*

CAVALRY

The samurai cavalryman would ride out against similarly mounted opponents with the spear gripped in the right hand, the left hand controlling the reins of the horse. By pushing his feet heavily into the stirrups, he would transfer some of the weight and momentum of the horse into the spear strike, hopefully sufficient to pierce a weaker point in the enemy armour, or to plunge the blade into the horse and bring the samurai down to earth. A greater challenge might actually come should the cavalryman be faced with swarming spear-armed infantrymen, whose principle objective was to strike up into the horse's stomach, throwing the rider, who could then be dispatched with multiple attacks. It was imperative that the mounted samurai keep the infantry at the maximum distance possible, sometimes by swinging the spear in a wide arc around the horse. He would also have trained himself to parry spears with his own.

The one element for which there was little defence was musketry, which threatened to end even the most elite samurai with nothing more than a stray musket ball. At the Battle of Nagashino, for example, Yamagata Masakage was one of the most formidable samurai in Takeda Shingen's army, noted for his weapon skills, tactical knowledge and his experience in battle. At one point, he rode fearlessly into combat against men of the Honda Tadakatsu, but volleys of musket fire brought both him and his horse crashing down before he could fight with steel. Having fallen from his horse, injured, Masakage was then enthusiastically beheaded by an opportunistic samurai.

◄ *A samurai helmet and half-face* menpō. *Note also the cord that tied the helmet to the head, known as the* shinobi-no-o. *(Vassil/CC-Zero)*

▼ *A detail of a piece of 17th-century mail armour. It was crucial to protect the forearms, which were a key target for quick sword slashes. (Vassil/CC-Zero)*

DISMOUNTED COMBAT

When dismounted samurai faced each other on the battlefield, it was on the basis on one-to-one combat, in an individual sword duel. The essence of the fight would be to avoid the opponent's strikes through nimble footwork, moving out of danger either through backward or oblique movements, while also parrying the sword blows. Ideally, the samurai's footwork would place him in the perfect position to make a powerful return strike, but often the first cuts would be lesser strikes, quickly made, to parts of the body such as hands, arms and legs – a disabling cut would be the prelude to a mortal one. Given that the samurai were so well armoured, a single killing blow at the outset was unlikely. Often, the blade strikes would cut armour lacing, gradually opening up vulnerable areas of the body beneath. Speed and fearlessness were essential in this fight to the death, which would ultimately end with the head of one of the warriors being separated from his body.

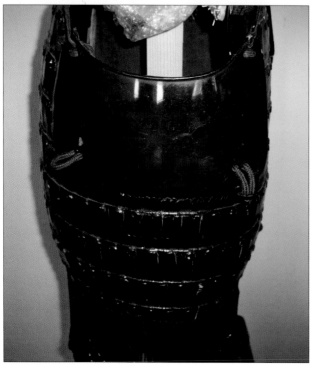

◄ *The armour covering a samurai's torso had to protect against both penetrating strikes and cutting slashes. (Samuraiantiqueworld/CC-BY-SA-3.0)*

CASE STUDY:

BATTLE OF NAGASHINO

The Battle of Nagashino, fought on 28 June 1575, is a fitting way to end this chapter, and indeed the book. Nagashino perfectly embodies the transition in Japanese warfare, from the old ways of the mounted samurai to the new ways of the arquebus-armed *ashigaru*. Although we should not overemphasise the originality of the battle – firearms had been used in many engagements already by this point in Japanese military history – the way that Oda Nobunaga applied these weapons to defeat a traditional samurai charge represents a primary shift in thinking, Nobunaga giving tactical privilege to his firearms and foot-mounted spearmen, rather than the samurai.

The origins of the battle lay in the siege of Nagashino Castle, located on the plain of Shidarahara in Mikawa Province. The lord of the castle, *daimyō* Okudaira Nobumasa, defected from allegiance to Takeda Shingen, shifting his

loyalties back over to the Tokugawa (their original affiliation, before Takeda muscle compelled a defection). In response, the Takeda sent an army of some 15,000 men, under command of Takeda Katsuyori, to besiege and reclaim the castle, the attacks beginning on 16 June. Despite the vice-like grip of the siege, Nobumasa still managed to send out messengers, who reached Okazaki Castle, capital of Mikawa, and found the ear of the great Oda Nobunaga and the equally luminary Tokugawa Ieyasu. Both pledged their help, and together raised a mighty army of 38,000 men.

After several days' march, the Nobunaga/Ieyasu army reached the edges of the siege, Katsuyori swinging most of his army, about 15,000 men, around to face this new threat that was forming up across the plain of Shidarahara. Katsuyori knew that the enemy held many arquebusiers – Nobunaga had some 3,000 matchlockmen in his ranks – but he felt that the recent heavy rain would have dampened their powder, leaving the admittedly larger opposing force vulnerable to a bold cavalry charge and foot assault. He arranged his forces into right flank, centre and left flank

▼ *A representation of the Battle of Nagashino, clearly showing Takeda Katsuyori's troops struggling against the barricaded enemy arquebusiers. (Tokugawa Art Museum/CC-PD-Mark)*

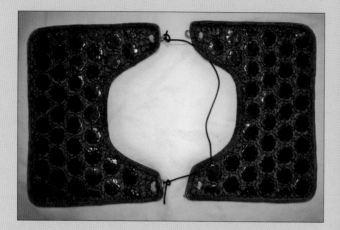

▲ *A pair of* kikko wakibiki *armour plates. These auxiliary plates were suspended over the armpit area as additional protection.* (Samuraiantiqueworld/CC-BY-SA-3.0)

▶ Kusazuri *were iron or leather plates hanging from the front and back of the* dō *to protect the lower body and upper leg.* (Samuraiantiqueworld/CC-BY-SA-3.0)

companies, each of between 3,000 and 4,000 men, with Katsuyori's HQ unit of 1,092 men just behind.

However, the Nobunaga/Ieyasu commanders were not relying on numbers alone to defeat the Takeda. Nobunaga expected a vigorous charge from his opponents, and looked to break it up like a wave smashing into a rock. He formed his lines just behind the Rengogawa, little more than a stream but with steep, slippery banks that would serve to slow the enemy horses down just in front of the Nobunaga/Ieyasu guns. To further retard the attack, Oda ordered the construction of a deep palisade, consisting of staggered lines of stakes. Behind these were his gunners, specifically arranged in groups of three to deliver rotating volley fire, one of the innovations of this battle. Furthermore, although the

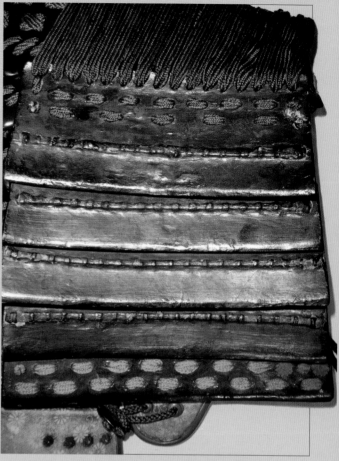

▼ *An illustration showing* ashigaru *using their matchlocks* (tanegashima) *from behind wooden shields* (tate), *an innovative early use of mobile cover.* (CC-PD-Mark)

◀ *One of outlandish* eboshi-*style* kabuto *helmets, based on designs worn by Shinto priests.* (Samuraiantiqueworld/ CC-BY-SA-3.0)

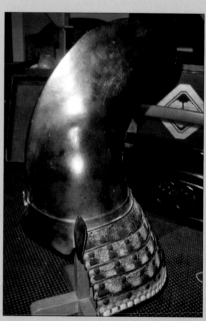

plain of Shidarahara was broad, Oda anchored his left flank on thick forest, reducing the length of line over which the fight would take place.

The Takeda attack came in the early light of 28 June, three mighty formations of Takeda troops moving down across the plain towards the Rengogawa. Just as Oda had predicted, the horses bunched up and slowed down as they crossed the stream, then as they emerged up the other bank and attempted to pick up speed again, the matchlockmen unleashed their rippling fire. (The momentum of the advance had already been slowed somewhat by the soft rice paddies on either side of the stream.) Rank by rank, the matchlockmen discharged their weapons into the enemy mass, horses, samurai and infantry dropping under the whistling rounds. For those enemy forces who managed to survive this fusillade and push forwards, they were met with both the palisade and also extra-long spears presented by the spearmen through the gaps, piercing horse and rider.

The initial Takeda attack was thus horribly blunted, with heavy casualties. But this was still just the beginning of a battle that would be fought for many hours. Although the arquebusiers certainly played a critical part in disrupting the opening attack, this did not prevent the action developing into many more traditional and brutal hand-to-hand clashes with sword and spear. Given the early casualties suffered by the Takeda, and the numerical superiority of the Nobunaga/Ieyasu army, the outcome was near inevitable. Of the 12,000 men Katsuyori pulled away from the siege lines to make the attack, 10,000 were killed, including 54 prominent samurai leaders.

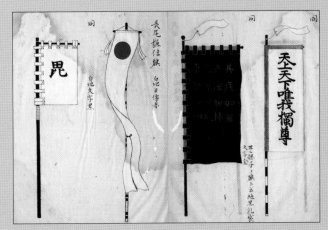

▲ Hata-jirushi *banners. On the far left is that of Takeda Shingen and on the far right that of Uesugi Kenshin. (Seiki Shuzu/CC-PD-Mark)*

Nagashino demonstrated that firearms, used rationally with tactics that compensated for their limitations, would be a deciding factor on the battlefield of the future. Because of Japan's subsequent isolationism, the way of the sword and spear would be integral to Japanese warfare for centuries yet, but the days of the samurai being at the vanguard of the army were disappearing. We can therefore draw a wavy line of connection between Nagashino and the tragic symbolism of the Satsuma Rebellion in 1877 (see page 25). Although those who fought at Nagashino would not be able to divine the future, the days of the samurai were thereafter numbered.

◄ *A modern samurai re-enactor shows the beauty and theatre of Japanese armour, in this case an ornate kabuto with a gilded crest. (Corpse Reviver/GFDL)*

SELECT BIBLIOGRAPHY

Absolon, Trevor (2017). *Samurai Armour: Volume I: The Japanese Cuirass*. Oxford: Osprey Publishing

Amdur, Ellis (2009). *Women Warriors of Japan: The Role of Arms-Bearing Women in Japanese History*. Koryu Books

Bottomley, Ian (2017). *Japanese Arms and Armour*. Leeds: Royal Armouries

Bryant, Anthony J. (1991). *Early Samurai: AD 200–1500*. Oxford: Osprey Publishing

Bryant, Anthony J. (2008). *The Samurai*. Oxford: Osprey Publishing

Clements, Jonathan (2010). *The Samurai: The Way of Japan's Elite Warriors*. London: Robinson

Coe, Michael et al. (2000). *Swords and Hilt Weapons*. London: Prion

Cummins, Antony and Minami, Yoshie (2013). *Samurai War Stories: Teachings and Tales of Samurai Warfare*. Stroud: The History Press

Cummins, Antony and Minami, Yoshie (2018). *The Book of Samurai: Samurai Arms, Armour & the Tactics of Warfare – The Collected Scrolls of Natori-ryu*. London: Watkins

Friday, Karl F. (2003). *Samurai, Warfare and the State in Early Medieval Japan*. London: Routledge

Irvine, Gregory (2000). *The Japanese Sword: The Soul of the Samurai*. London: V&A Publications

Miyamoto Musashi (1993). *The Book of Five Rings*. Trans. Thomas Cleary. Boston, MA: Shambhala

Nitobe, Izanō (1908). *Bushido: The Soul of Japan*. 13th edition. Tokyo: Teibi

Smart, Ninian (1971). *The Religious Experience of Mankind*. London: Collins

Turnbull, Stephen (2010). *Ashigaru 1467–1649*. Oxford: Osprey Publishing

Turnbull, Stephen (2006). *Hatamoto: Samurai Hose and Foot Guards 1540–1724*. Oxford: Osprey Publishing

Turnbull, Stephen (1979). *Samurai Armies 1500–1615*. Oxford: Osprey Publishing

Turnbull, Stephen (2001). *The Book of the Samurai: The Warrior Class of Japan*. Rochester: Grange

Turnbull, Stephen (2016). *The Samurai*. Oxford: Osprey Publishing

Turnbull, Stephen (2010). *The Samurai and the Sacred*. Oxford: Osprey Publishing

Turnbull, Stephen (2000). *The Samurai Sourcebook*. London: Cassell & Co

Turnbull, Stephen (2005). *Warriors of Medieval Japan*. Oxford: Osprey Publishing

Wong, Charles A. (1939). *Bible of the World*. Ed. Robert D. Ballou. New York

Yamamoto Tsunetomo (1983). *Hagakure: The Book of the Samurai*. Trans. William Scott Wilson. Tokyo: Kondasha International

ENDNOTES

1   Inazo– 1908: 3–4
2   Bryant 2008: 19
3   Turnbull 2016: 48
4   Turnbull 2016: 48
5   Yamamoto 1983: 33
6   Turnbull 2016: 58
7   Yamamoto 1983: 41
8   Ibid
9   Ibid 25
10 Turnbull 2016: 59
11 Yamamoto 1983: 164
12 Cummins 2018: 210–11
13 Wong 1939: 404
14 Miyamoto 1993: 16
15 Munenori, in Miyamoto 1993: 68
16 Cummins 2018: 208
17 Munenori, in Miyamoto 1993: 71
18 Wong 1939: 472
19 Yamamoto 1983: 18–19
20 Turnbull 2000: 303
21 Bryant 2008: 52
22 Bottomley 2017: 54
23 Miyamoto 1993: 13
24 Ellis 2009: np
25 Miyamoto 1993: 20
26 Turnbull 2000: 137
27 Turnbull 2000: 138
28 Turnbull 2000: 151
29 Turnbull 2000: 153
30 Ibid
31 Cummins 2018: 37
32 Cummins 2018: 28
33 Cummins 2013: n.p.
34 Turnbull 2016: 156
35 Cummins 2018: 244
36 Ibid 115
37 Turnbull 2010: 18
38 Cummins 2018: 12–13. Note that the source of the Chinese formations is given as Sun-Tzu.
39 Turnbull 2000: 272
40 Turnbull 2000: 25
41 Zōhyō Monogatari, np
42 Zōhyō Monogatari, np
43 Turnbull 2000: 168

INDEX

Please note that Japanese names have been indexed as they appear in the text, without being inverted. Page numbers in **bold type** refer to illustrations/captions only, with no accompanying information in the main text.

afterlife 53
agemaki 74
Akashi Gidayu **61**
Akechi Mitsuhide **147**
Akugenta Yoshihara 119
alcoves 32
Alternate Attendance System 22–3
Amaterasu 52
Analects 54
ancestor worship 52–3
archers/archery 58, 88–90, 105, 140–2
Arima Toyouji **138**
arm armour 75–6, **121**
armour **9**, **51**, **57**, 68–83, **111**, **117**, **130**, **135**
   for horses **113**, **119**
   ō-yoroi **64**, 71–3, 78, **81**
arquebusiers/arquebus 102–5, 140–2
   Battle of Nagashino 149–51
arrow-carrying servants 120–1
arrowhead formation 133
arrows 88–9
Asai Hisamasa 64
Asai Nagamasa 64
Asakura Yoshikage 64
Asano Takumi-no-Kami Naganori 66
ase nagashi no ana **72**
ashigaru 78, 109–10
   command structure 131
   punishments 113
   weapons 86–7, 94, 102–3, 105, **150**
Ashikaga shogunate 18–19, 21
Ashikaga Takauji 17–18
   armour of **117**
Ashikaga Yoshimasa 19
   cha no yu tea ceremony 40
atarikuji 112
auxiliary armour 77
Azuma Kagami 39

backplates 75
baggage trains 122–3
bamboo tea whisk 41
banners **125**, **126–7**, 138–9, **151**
batsuho 112–13
battle formations 132–5
Battle of Akasaka **120**
Battle of Fujito **129**
Battle of Hakodate 24
Battle of Ishibashiyama 14
Battle of Kawanakajima 63, 65, 136–7
Battle of Koromogawa 14
Battle of Kurikara 14

Battle of Mikata ga Hara **18**
Battle of Minatogawa 17
Battle of Nagashino 63, **147**, 149–51
Battle of Sekigahara 11, 22–3, **122**
Battle of Tabaruzaka **25**
Battle of Yamazaki **114**
battlefield command 138–9
battlefield flags and banners **125**, **126–7**, 138–9, **151**
battlefield rituals 54
beards 36–7
behaviour 112–13
biwa lute **45**
board games 45
body hair 37
bokuto **6**, **100**, 101
Book of Five Rings, The 8, 55, 59, 86–7
Books of the Dead/Injured 64
boots 34
bows and archery 58, 88–90, 105, 140–2
   bowman sergeants 116, 142
box-carrying servants 116, 120
breastplates 70–1, 73–5, 78–80, 83, **113**
breech-loading cannon **145**
breeches 34
Buddhism 56–8
   temples **28**, **48–9**, 55
bugyo 131
bullet-box-carrying servants 121
bumaru 121
bunbu ichi 43
bunraku theatre 45–6
bushidō 7–9
Byōdō-in Buddhist temple **28**

calligraphy 43–4
campaign headquarters 111–12
camps 125
cannon 145
castles 28–31
catapults 102
cavalry 147
cha no yu tea ceremony 40–2
chain armour **111**, **148**
chasen **41**
chasitsu 41–2
chest armour *see* breastplates
Chinese gunpowder weapons 102
choda formation 133
chodo 125
chonmage 36
chu (Confucian concept) 56, 61
chuzai punishments 112–13
classical-era armour 70–7
clogs 34–5
clothing 34–5
coats 34
codes of discipline 112
collecting heads 64

combat formations 132–5
command centres 125
command structure 128–30
   on the battlefield 138–9
conch shells 110, **117**, 139
Confucianism 54–6
construction of swords 96–8
cooking 125
courtesans 47
crane's wing formation 133
crescent moon formation 133
crimson foliage hit 101
cultural understanding 7–8

Dai-o 40
dai-shogun 129
daimyō **6**, 20, 24, 43, 108, 128–9
daisho **95**, **96**, **99**
Date Masamune 80
death 60–7
death poems 63, 67
dining etiquette 39
discipline 112, 131
disease 42
dismounted combat 148
divine wind 65
dō breastplate 70–1, 73–5, 78–80, 83, **113**
dō-maru 74–5, 78
drain hole (in helmets) **72**
drawing of lots 112
dress 34–5
drink 40–2 *see also* water
drums 114, 139
dwellings 28–33

eboshi kabuto 82
Edo (city) **13**, **26–7**, **29**
Edo Neo-Confucianism 55
Edo period 22–3
ema 53, **55**
Emperor Go-Daigo 16–18
Emperor Go-Toba 15
Emperor Meiji 24
Emperor Nijō **124**
Emperor Ōjin 110
enlightenment 57–8
Enryaku-ji (temple) 13
etchu zunari shikoro 80
etchubo face masks 82
etiquette, dining 39
everyday dress 34–5
evolution of armour 78–83
Exclusion Edict (1639) 23
experience of battle 140–8
expiatory suicide 63, 65

face masks **57**, **60**, 77, 80, 82–3, **140**, **145**
facial hair 36–7
Family Traditions on the Art of War 8, 55

female samurai 92
fighting techniques 99, 101
filial piety (Confucian concept) 56
finishing of swords 98
fire and its prevention 33, **144**
fire-lances 102
firearms 102–5
fish 39
fish scales formation 133
flags **125**, **126–7**, 138–9, **151**
fletching 88
flutes 45
flying geese formation 133
folding (in swordmaking) 97
food 38–9
   siege warfare 144–5
   when on campaign 124–5
foot soldiers *see ashigaru*
footwear 34–5, **37**
foraging parties 124
forehead armour 73
forming swords 97–8
47 Ronin **19**, 66
fourth Battle of Kawanakajima 63, 65, 136–7
fruit 39
Fujiwara family 12
Fujiwara no Hidesato **58**
Fujiwara no Michinaga **47**
Fujiwara no Nobuyori 12
fukigaeshi 73, **81**
fuku-shogun 129
fundoshi 34
furniture 32–3
Fushimi Momoyama Castle 30

Game of Generals 45
ganko formation 133
geta 34–5
gezai punishments 112–13
go 45
go fudai karo-shu 130
Go-Daigo, Emperor 16–18
Go-Toba, Emperor 15
Gorin no sho see *Book of Five Rings, The*
goshinrui-shu 130
Great Learning, The 55
green tea 40–2
grooming 36–7, **122**
grooms (for horses) 118–19
guard positions for sword fighting 101
gunbai war fans 115
gunbaisha 54
Gunboryo document 129
gungen 129
gunpowder weapons 102
gunsen war fans 115
gunso 129
guruwa 77
gyorin formation 133

habaki 98
hachi 72–3
hachimaki 36
Hachiman (war god) 72, 110
Hagakure 37, 43–4, 60–1, 99
    advice on death 51
    notes on being a *kaishakukin* 63
haidate 76, **79**
hair 36–7, 82, 122
hakama 34–5
hammering (in swordmaking) 97
hamon lines **97**, 98
hanbo face masks 82
hand guards (for swords) 98
hane 88
Hangaku Gozen **141**
haori 34
happuri face masks 82, **83**
hara-kiri see *seppuku*
haramaki-dō 75, 78
hardening of swords 98
hari bachi kabuto 80
hasamibako mochi 116, 120
hata-jirushi 139, **151**
Hatakeyama Shigetada **143**
hatamoto 128, 131
hatamoto shoyakunin 130
hayago 103
head collecting 64
head-shaped helmets 80, 82
headbands 36
Heian period 12
Heieki Yoho 51, 54–5, 128–9
Heiji Insurrection 12
Heike Monogatari 92
helmets 59, 72–3, 80–2, **131**, **148**,
    150–1
high command 128–30
hilltop castles 28
hilts (of swords) 98
Himeji Castle 28–30
hinero shikoro 80
hirajiro 28–9
hirayamajiro 28
Hishikawa Moronobu 47
hiso 102
hitatare 34
hoen formation 133
Hōgen Insurrection 12, **132**
Hōjō clan 17
Hōjō Masako 58, 92
Hōjō Sōun 33, 35, 36
Hōjō Tokimasa 15
Hōjō Tokimune 16
Hōjō Uijyasa 20, 21
Hōjō Ujimasa 67
Hōjō Ujitsuna 102
hon iyozane maru dō **71**, **79**
hon maru 31
honjin 125, 128
Honno-ji Incident **147**
horns (on helmets) 73, **81**
horo 138
horse armour **113**, **119**
horses 118–19, **120**, **141**, 147, 151
hoshi formation 133
Hosokawa clan 19
hotoke 53
hotoke-dō 79–80, **83**
household rules 43

Ibaraki-doji **15**
ichiban kubi 146
ikusa-bugyo 129

inuoumono 90
Itsukushima Shrine **45**
Iyonojo Muntesugu **97**

Japanese bow 88–90
Jidai Matsuri Festival of Ages **109**
jigai 62–3
jikishindan 130
jinkai 110, **117**, 139
jo-shogun 129
jumonji yari 94
junshi 65
jusha 55–6
juzai punishments 112–13

kabuki theatre 45–6
kaburi-ya 89
kabuto 72–3, 80, 82, **120**, **131**,
    150–1
kachi-gashira 117
kaishakukin 63
Kajiwara Kagesue **143**
kakun 43
kakuyoku formation 133
Kamakura *bakufu* 14–17
Kamata Masakiyo 119
Kamei Koremi **57**
kami 32, 110
    Shinto religion 52–3
kamidana 53
kamikaze tactics 67
kamishimo 34
Kanmu Taira clan 12
Kano Yosaburo 45
karimata forked arrowheads 89
karuta tatami dō **83**
kashindan 128
Kasugayama Castle **144**
kataginu 34
katana 6, **86**, 95–6, **97–8**
katana kake **99**
katanagatari 109
Kato Heizaburo 42
Kato Kiyomasa **19**, 42, 82
Katsukawa Shunsho 47
Katsura Rikyu Imperial Villa **33**
kawagane 97
kazaori-eboshi 82
kebiki odoshi 73, 78
kegutsu 34
kemari 46
key virtues of the samurai 9
keyhole formation 133
Ki Castle **52**
Kichinaizaemon 120
Kikkawa Tsuneie 144
kikko manchira 77
kikko wakibiki **150**
kimono 34
Kira Kozuke-no-Suke Yoshinaka 66
kisha 90
Kiso horses 118, **120**
ko (Confucian concept) 56
ko-uma-jirushi 139
kobokama 34
Kōfuku-ji Buddhist temple **55**
kogake 77
koicha 41
Kojima Yatar **8**
Kokin Wakash 6
koku (rice measure) 38
Komokuten **51**
Kongorikishi 55
konida bugyo 123

konida tsuzura no koto 123
Kosaka Danjo Masanobu 136–7
koshiate 78, 96
koshirae **95**
kote 75–6
koyaku formation 133
Kōyō Gunkan 108, 130
Kublai Khan 16, **108**
kumi uchi no komyo 146
K'ung 54–6
kuni-shu 130, 132
kura no koto 118–19
kurawa 31
kuribuki 135
kurikomi 135
Kuroda Yoshitaka **115**
kusari gusoku **111**
kusazuri 73–4, 79, **150**
Kusunoki Masashige 16–17
kutsu 34
kuwagata 73
kuzurekiwa no komyo 146
kyo bows 88
Kyoho famine 38
Kyoto (city) 18–19, 21–2

labourers 121
lacing of armour 73, **81**
lacquering of armour 73
Lao Tzu 59
load-carrying 120–2
logistics 120–3
loincloth 34
long snake formation 133
loyalty (Confucian concept) 56
loyalty in death 60–1, 65

mabisashi 73
maedate **59**, **81**
Maede Toshiie 82
mail armour **111**, 148
maki-e go game board **22**
making swords 96–8
maku 111–12, 128
manchira 77
manju no wa **35**, 77
marching 114–16
maritime warfare **146**
matchlock weapons **87**, 102–5, **142**
meat 39
medical care 140
Meiji Restoration 24–5
Meimei-an tea house **42**
men yoroi face masks 82
menpō face masks **57**, 82, **135**, **140**,
    145, 148
messengers 138
military secretaries 64
millet 38–9
Minamoto family 12–15
Minamoto Kiso no Yoshinaka 14
Minamoto no Kanetsuna 13
Minamoto no Nakatsuna 13
Minamoto no Sanetomo 15
Minamoto no Ta 63
Minamoto no Tomonaga 119
Minamoto no Yoriie 15
Minamoto no Yorimasa 63
Minamoto no Yoritomo 12–15, 39,
    145
Minamoto no Yoshitomo 12
Minamoto no Yoshitsune 12, 14, **67**
minotenari formation 135
'Mirror of the East' 39

Miyamoto Musashi **6**, 8, 55, 59, 86–7,
    99, 101
mobile campaign headquarters
    111–12
mobilisation of troops 110–11
mochi 39
Mochihito, Prince 13
mochiyari katsugi 116, 120
mochizutsu 116
mogami-dō 78
Mōko Shōrai Ekotoba **138**, **141**
mon 138
Mongol invasions 16, 86, **108**, **120**
monks 13, 40, 57
Mōri Hidemoto **122**
mountain castles 28–30
mounted archery 90
moustaches 37
muenbotoke 52
Munechika **53**
Muromachi period 18–19
music and musicians 45, 114, 125
    battlefield command 139
musket sergeants 116
musket-carrying servants 116
muskets 102–5, 140–2
    protection from 78
mustering of armies 110
Myochin Ki no Munesada **121**

Nabeshima clan 43
nagako 97–8
nagamaki 93
naginata **87**, 91–3
Nakamura Shikan **147**
Nakano Takeko 92
Nanbokuchō Wars 16–18
Nara period 12
Natori Masazumi 8–9, 55
Natori-ryu 8–9
    baggage train management 123
    battle formations 134–5
    collecting heads 64
    four basic areas of study 59
    Heieki Yoho 51, 128–9
    kisa-bugyo duties 129–30
    kura no koto saddles 118–19
    music on the battlefield 139
    samurai selection 109
    Scroll of Heaven 112
    security 116–17
neck armour 73, 77, 80, 82
ni-mai-dō 79
Nichiren Buddhism 42, 57
nijiriguchi 41
Nijō, Emperor **124**
ningyo joruri theatre 45–6
ninja 131
nirvana 57
Nishikawa Castle **33**
Nitobe Inazo 8, 9
Nitta Yoshisada 17
nobori 139
nodowa 77
noh theatre 45–6
noroshi towers 111

o-uma-jirushi 138–39
ō-yoroi armour **64**, 71–3, 78, **81**
Oba Kagechika 14
obi 35
ochoko 40
Oda Nobunaga 20–2, 30, 53, 63–4,
    102, **123–4**, **147**, 149–51

odachi 93
Odawara Hojo Godai Festival **7**
Odawara (priest) 102
Ōishi Yoshio Kuranosuke **62**, 66
Ōjin, Emperor 110
okegawa-dō 79
Okudaira Nobumasa 149
Onin War 19
onna-bugeisha 92
oration 43
order of marching 114
oshidaiko 114
Oū Eikei Gunki 144
Oyamada Nobushige 63

pace of marching 114, 116
paper screens 31–3
pastimes 43–7
peace treaties, enforced suicide
    65–7
Period of Warring States *see* Sengoku
    jidai
Perry, Commodore Matthew 24
personal equipment 121–2
personal load-carrying 120–2
pillaging 112, 124
pitfall traps 125
plains castles 28–9
poetry 44
    death poems **63**, 67
polishing of swords 98
pre-march rituals 110–12
Prince Mochihito 13
prostitution 47
public shame 63, 65
punishments 65–7, 112–13
purification rituals 54

quivers 89, **105**

Rape of Nanjing 67
re-enactments **7**, 57, **68–9**, **104–5**
reisei men face masks 82
religion 52–9
renga 44
rice 38–9, 124–5
riding boots 34
rituals 54
    pre-march 110–12
    suicide 62–7
rokuji 129
ronin 36
    47 Ronin **19**, 66

saddles 118–19
Saigo Takamori **14**, 112
Sakanoue no Tamuramaro 67
sakayaki 36, 82
sake 40
sakikata-shu 130
saku formation 133
Samurai Sourcebook 104–5
samurai swords *see* swords
samurai-daishō 129
sandal-carrying servants 116
sandals 34, **37**
Sannosai Festival **57**
Sasaki Moritsuna **129**
Sasaki Takatsuna **143**
sashimono identifier **15**, **123**, 139
satori 57–8
Satsuma Rebellion 25, **146**
saya (scabbards) 91, 98
scouts 116–18

Scroll of Heaven 112, 114
seafood 39
seconds (for *seppuku*) 63
security 116–18, 123, 128
sei ita 75
Sen no Rikyu 40
sendai-dō 80
Sengaku-ji temple 66
Sengoku *jidai* 20–3, 29
    rise of female samurai 92
Senshi no ho 109
seppuku **14**, **61**, 62–7
servants 116, 120–1
Seven-Layered Formation 134–5
shamisen **39**
sharpening of swords 98
shaving of hair 82
Shibaraku (play) **46**
Shigisan Castle 29–30
shikoro 73, 80
shin armour 76
shinai 101
shinboku **53**
shingane 97
shinobi no mono 131
Shinto religion 52–4
Shintogo Kunimitsu 96
shirasaya **95–6**
shirei 53
shodo 44
shoes 34–5, **37**
shogi 45
shogun/shogunate 6, 12–15,
    20, 129
shoji 31–3
Shokin-tei tea pavilion **33**
shoulder armour 74, 79, **121**
Siege of Akasaka Castle **17**
Siege of Hara Castle **23**
Siege of Hataya Castle 144
Siege of Odara Castle 113
Siege of Osaka **24**
Siege of Ulsan **110**, **137**
siege warfare 144–5
signal fires 111, 136
sliding paper screens 31–3
smelting (in swordmaking) 96–7
sninobi-no-o **148**
social ranks 108–9
socks 34, 77
sode 74, 79, **121**
sode-jirushi **139**
sohei 13, 57
sokotsu-shi 63, 65
somen face masks **60**, 82
spear-carrying servants 116, 120
spearmen 142–3
spirits 32, 52–3, 110
standards *see* banners
strike points for sword fighting 101
stringed instruments 45
sugake odoshi 73, 78
suicide **14**, **61**, 62–7
suji bachi kabuto 80
suneate 76
sword hangers **78**, 96
swords 93, 95–101

tabi 34
tachi 95–6
Taira family 12–14
Taira no Kiyomori 12–14
Taira no Masakado 12
Taira no Tomomori 63

Takamatsu Castle **33**
Takeda Katsuyori **58**, 63, 149–51
Takeda Shingen 20–1, 149
    fourth Battle of Kawanakajima
    136–7
Tales of the Foot Soldiers see
    Zōhyō Monogatari
tamabako mochi 121
tamahagane 96
tanegashima **87**
tangs 97–8
tantō **63**, **87**, 96
Tao Te Ching 59
Taoism 59, 111
tatami dō **146**
tatami mats 32
tate-eri 77
tea and its ceremonies 40–2
tehen 72
Tenkei Rebellion 12
teppo ashigaru kogashira 116,
    140–2
teppo ko gashira 103
tessen war fans 115
theatre 45–6
thigh armour **76**, **79**
throat armour 77
thunder-crash bombs 102
tokonoma 32, 41
Tokugawa clan, family crest **54**
Tokugawa Ieyasu 20–2, **36**, 63, 102,
    113, 149–51
Tokugawa shogunate 7, 22–4
    endorsement of *go* 45
Tokugawa Tsunayoshi 66
Tomoe Gozen **36**, 92, **143**
topknots 36–7
torii 44, 53
Torii Mototada 61
tosei-gusoku 75, **76**, 78–80
Tottori Castle **30**
Toyotomi clan, emblem of **116**
Toyotomi Hideyoshi 22, **65**, 67, 109,
    115, 144
training methods for sword fighting
    99, 101
troops, types of 116
True Pure Land Buddhism 57
tsuba 98
tsukai-ban 138
tsuranaki 34
tsurubashiri 73
Turnbull, Stephen 32, 104–5, 122,
    137
21 Articles of Hōjō Sōun 33, 35, 36

uagane 97
uchigatana 96
Uesugi Kagekatsu 63
Uesugi Kenshin 20–1, 44, **63**, **108**,
    144
    fourth Battle of Kawanakajima
    136–7
umajirushi 114, **125**, **138**
umatori 118–19
urushi lacquering 73
Usa Jingū Shinto shrine 56
usucha 41
utsubo quiver 89
Utsunomiya Castle **31**

vegetables 39
vest, armoured 77
virtues 9

wabi-cha tea ceremony 40–1
waidate 73
waist sashes 35
wakibaki 77
wakidate tsunamoto **137**
wakizashi **95**, 96, **98**
Wanatabe no Tsuna **15**
wangetsu formation 133
war banners **126–7**
war fans 115
war shells 110
waraji 34, **37**
warrior monks 13, 57
Wars Between the Courts 16
washing 36
water 125
    siege warfare 144–5
Way of Death, the 61–2
Way of Selecting Samurai 109
Way of Tea, the 40–2
weapons 86–105
Wendelin Boeheim 72
wind-folded *eboshi* 82
winnowing fan formation 135
wooden swords **100**, 101
World War II 25, 67
wounded soldiers 140
written arts 44

ya no ye arrowheads 89
yabako mochi 120–1
yabusame 90
Yagyu Munemori 8, 55, 58
Yamagata Masakage 147
yamajiro 28–30
Yamamoto Kansuke 136–7
Yamamoto Tsunetomo 8, 37, 43–4,
    60–1
    notes on being a *kaishakukin* 63
Yamana clan 19
Yamato government 12
yanagi-ba arrowheads 89
yari 94
yashiki 31–2
Yin-Yang 59
yodarekake 82
yoke formation 133
yokome 131
Yoshiwara district 47
yuhitsu 64
Yukimori **76**
yumi ashigaru kogashira 116, 142
yumi bows **24**, 88

Zen Buddhism 41–2, 56–8
    acceptance of death 60
Zenkō-ji Buddhist temple **48–9**
Zhu Xi 55
Zōhyō Monogatari 8, 119–21
    advice on food and water 124–5
    battlefield insights 141–3
zonae 132, 134
zoritori 116
zunari kabuto 80, 82